HOW TO WRITE A WILL

DON'T LET THE STATE WRITE YOUR WILL FOR YOU

GLORIA DAWKINS ISAAC

ISBN: 978-1-7328668-6-7
ISBN: 978-1-7328668-2-9

Layout: Wade Hunkin / Retrodiction Publication Design Services

Book Cover: Alfanso Fraser / falfanso@gmail.com

To contact the publisher: hello@toproadpublishing.com

DEDICATION

I dedicate this book to my parents, the late Lloyd H. Simpson JP, and the late Lilian Vivian Simpson. Since I was a child, my father worked hard, planned and built an estate for his family. He always had a current will in place. His jovial "Beware of the pen," reminded my siblings and me to be on our best behavior and walk the narrow path, as his pen could easily remove us from his will.

My dad was a patriot, a community man, a politician, a family man, and a disciplinarian. He always kept current on financial matters. Once an occurrence would affect his portfolio, he was off to sit with his lawyers to effect any necessary changes.

With her quiet strength, my mother managed one of the family businesses. Her work ethic, multi-talented nature, and dedication to the family left us a legacy of self-reliance and kindness to others.

I am thankful to my late parents for the legacy they left us. They demonstrated their beliefs and set an example for us to emulate. I constantly reflect on their selflessness, inner strength, boldness, courage, and the sacrifices they bore for our family.

At times, I cannot help but focus on how they faced hard work and challenging times with dignity while finding joy in giving back to their community. Their lives and legacy have brought meaning to my life.

My dear parents, your legacy lives on, and now it is our turn to pass it on.

I will always love you both! All the beautiful memories will forever be in my heart.

Create your legacy and pass the baton

Billie Jean King

ACKNOWLEDGMENT

Special thanks to the management and the rest of the team at Electronic Forms LLC (eforms.com) for allowing me to use samples of their legal forms as illustrations in this book. Thanks too to caring.com for the use of the statistics from their survey.

My appreciation.

The contribution of the team of talented experts who ensured a professional outcome is sincerely acknowledged:
Editors: Michelle Neita & Winston E. Hobson, Esq. (Legal)
Proofreader: Dawn Lindo
Graphic Artists: Alfanso Fraser (Book cover) Wade Hunkin (Layout)
Together we made it happen. Great things happen when we work together to create awareness and positive results.

Thank you very much.

To my family and friends who believed in me and supported me throughout the process, you kept me focused and persistent to the very end. I hope I make you proud.

Thanks for the push.

Together you all have helped to make it happen! I appreciate you!

WHY YOU SHOULD READ THIS BOOK

"It is up to us to live up to the legacy that was left for us, and to leave a legacy that is worthy of our children and of future generations."

Christine Gregoire

Thanks for purchasing this book. It is for persons who love and care for others enough during their lifetime that they would want to ensure that their loved ones continue to experience that love and care, even after their passing. That legacy lives on, and those persons are never forgotten.

I hope this book will guide you through the steps in writing a simple will or getting you more prepared to converse with an attorney or estate planner who will prepare your more complex will. The highlighted elements and requirements of a will should help ensure the distribution of your legacy to the beneficiaries of your choice.

Most of us have something that we own. Death is a sure road for all of us, and since we cannot take our worldly possessions with us, we should prepare for the orderly distribution of our hard-earned assets to our intended beneficiaries. We choose to write a will and have our desires implemented, or die without a will, *dying intestate*, and give the state the authority to distribute our legacy to beneficiaries based on the law. The latter might not result in the preferred beneficiaries receiving their intended legacy.

Today, more people realize the importance of having a current will, yet many do not have one in place. In a 2021 survey conducted by **caring.com**, the study found that despite the COVID-19 pandemic increasing the desire to write a will, 2 out of 3 Americans still do not have estate planning documents in place. Surprisingly, the study found that younger adults are 63% more likely to have a will now, while middle-aged and older adults are less likely to have one than pre-pandemic figures. The study also shows that 18-34 year-olds are now 16% more likely to have a will than persons in the 35-54 age group. (https://www.caring.com/caregivers/estate-planning/wills-survey). In some places, there is a myth that once someone writes a will, he will die shortly after that. There is no truth in this, as many persons have had their wills in place for several years, updating them as they see fit.

In the United States, many laws differ by state. In addition to Federal laws, the individual states, each being a sovereign entity, can create and enforce their constitutional laws based on their needs. Laws relating to the writing of wills can therefore be handled differently by state, making it necessary to be aware of the rules in a jurisdiction.

This book serves as a guide to cover the contents and preparation of a will and discusses other instruments for consideration as part of your overall estate planning. It covers general rules for writing a will. You may choose to write your own will for a smaller and uncomplicated estate, but an attorney or financial planner should prepare wills for larger and more complex estates. Gathering the necessary information for preparing a will makes for an informed and comprehensive discussion with the will preparer.

To demonstrate the similarities and differences in some of the rules of law on different topics, the examples, samples, and templates used are from Florida, the United States, and Jamaica, West Indies.

My experience as a life insurance salesperson exposes me to both sides of the fence, witnessing families benefit from legacies left in a will, and families that suffer the consequences of a breadwinner dying intestate. Of significance is the exposure of negative behavior in some families on the death of their loved ones, especially when a will is not in place. During these already challenging and stressful times, many persons are disappointed with the family rifts that result and continue afterward.

As a life insurance agent, I spend time protecting families and businesses from financial disaster by delivering checks to beneficiaries on the death of their breadwinners. I have qualified for all major sales awards in Jamaica and the Caribbean, the Million Dollar Round Table (MDRT), which is a club for the top one percent (1%) of life insurance agents across the world, while serving the industry in various capacities, helping people voluntarily. As someone who always believes in furthering my studies to serve my clients at the highest level towards achieving their financial goals, I studied and earned the Chartered Life Underwriter (CLU) designation, which covers insurance and business-related topics and estate planning. I was able to complete simple wills for my clients and put them in touch with qualified attorneys or estate planners to get their more complex wills done. I also served as an executive, heading the sales and marketing team in a life insurance company and helping to influence policy for the betterment of agents and policyholders.

Motivation to write this book originated from a blog that I posted on social media, which received encouraging feedback. In public and private messages, many people thanked me for the tips. Some even admitted to not having a will in place and promised to get one done to protect their families.

I have shared stories that have remained etched in my memory, with the names changed to protect the families' privacy. I hope that readers will benefit from the information gleaned from this book and realize that writing a will is an essential and valuable gift to their families.

Procrastination is not an option for getting your will done and, if you already have one, to having it reviewed and updated.

Once again, thanks for purchasing this book, happy reading, and let us get this critical "must-do" done today!

Gloria Dawkins Isaac

In praise of

"How to write a will.... DON'T let the state write your will for you."

I am pleased to write a note supporting this book, which I believe the readers will find quite helpful, informative, and as interesting as I did. I anticipate the readers will range from laypeople to lawyers, estate planners, insurance agents, and others looking for answers to questions relating to managing one's affairs while alive to ensure matters get handled as desired after death.

This book may be considered a beginner's guide or a broad overview of the topic(s) stated in the contents. The matter has been well researched and set out. Every page is informative, and readers will be left knowing they have just come across beneficial information. Because of this aspect of the book, some may consider it a sort of "how-to" guide in these areas.

While the book speaks of a broad topic, it goes into specific details as they are applied in certain jurisdictions, enabling those persons to find the information especially useful. It also references certain information for readers, allowing them to seek additional information if desired.

It would help if you always kept it close at hand as a starter (and even beyond) for questions related to wills and estate planning or as a source to prepare you for your first visit to a lawyer and estate planner.

Again, I am pleased to have the opportunity to write this note about an exciting book that covers a matter that is especially important or should be to everyone. **Everybody needs to read this book.**

Winston E. Hobson, Esq.

Orlando, Florida

In praise of

"How to write a will.... DON'T let the state write your will for you"

Although not intended for legal advice, this book is an easy read for anyone with assets. It is not just for the wealthy, but anyone with a bank account, a home, a car, a 401k, or other pension funds will benefit from it. The language is simple yet specific enough to spark interest.

The stories and examples hit the mark! I speak mainly of the case where an unintended beneficiary received the lion's share of an estate because of the wording of the will by someone who had no idea of the future value of his estate and who had not updated his will. The information and advice in this book could have helped such an individual, but it is not too late for anyone in a similar position to benefit from it.

A path is laid out for planning your legacy, it guides you on how to write your will, and the stories from the author's experience provide the necessary motivation for getting it done NOW!

Gloria correctly suggests involving an attorney or estate planner, especially for larger and more complex estates. She helps you prepare for a quicker and more thorough meeting with your attorney or estate planner. This, hopefully, will reduce the meeting time and possibly the cost of getting your will written.

I have been in the insurance and investment industries for over 45 years and highly recommend this book. More importantly, through this book, Gloria will affect many lives, and for that, she should be justly proud. Good luck to her.

Pat Billera

Trainer at a major school in the tri-county area

In praise of

"How to write a will.... DON'T let the state write your will for you"

Congratulations to the author for an excellent and critically important publication.

This well-researched guide will be welcomed by many. It not only provides needed information but it does so with simplicity, empathy, and care. The reader is fully engaged as the author's experiences buttress her conviction that wills and estate planning are fundamental to generational well-being and ongoing development. The "real-life" cases she includes perfectly demonstrate this.

Gloria has written a powerful and helpful book. It enlightened me during proofreading and will be a similar beacon for all who purchase it.

Dawn Lindo

Proofreader

DEDICATION i
ACKNOWLEDGMENT iii
WHY YOU SHOULD READ THIS BOOK iv

CHAPTER 1 **WHY WRITE A WILL?** 1
What is a will? 1
The importance of writing a will 1
Protecting family 2
Protecting estates 3
Protecting minor children 3
Caring for someone with special needs 3
Preparing for an unmarried spouse 3
Planning for blended families 4
Unlisted beneficiaries 4
Protecting businesses 4
Saving on inheritance and estate taxes 4
Contributing to charity 5
Disinheriting heirs 5
Disinheriting children 5
Disinheriting a spouse 5
Forgiving debts 6
Donating organs 6
Caring for pets 6

CHAPTER 2 **WHAT CONSTITUTES A VALID WILL?** 9
Types of wills 9
Formats of a will 9
Stipulations of a valid will 10

CHAPTER 3 **CONTENTS OF A WILL** 13
Parties to a Will 13
Checklist for consideration in writing a will 13
Executor 14
Beneficiaries 15
Guardian 15
Trustee 15
Gifts to minors under Florida Law 16
Gifts to minors in Jamaica 16
Assets and Liabilities 16
Other elements to consider 17
Bank accounts 17
Property ownership 18
Types of transfers of property 18
Other assets 18
Digital assets 19
Naming the beneficiaries 21
What should be included in a will 21
What should not be included in a will 22
Completion of the will 23
Who signs a will? 23
Dating a will 23

CHAPTER 4 **DEATH DUTIES/ESTATE TAXES** 25
Death taxes in Florida 25
Death duties in Jamaica 26

CHAPTER 5 **INTESTACY & PROBATE** 31
Intestacy in Florida 31
Probate in Florida 33
Duties of the Personal Representative 33
Duties of the Trustee 34
The application 35
Types of probate 35
The process 36
Intestacy in Jamaica 38
The process 40
Application for the Grant of Letters of Administration 40
Probate in Jamaica 40

CHAPTER 6 **READY TO PREPARE A SIMPLE WILL?** 43
Reminders 43
Collecting the data for a simple will 46
Will templates 52

CHAPTER 7 **PREPPING FOR YOUR ESTATE PLANNING MEETING** 55
Preparation notes for an estate 56

CHAPTER 8 **FOR DISCUSSION WITH YOUR ESTATE PLANNER/ATTORNEY** 79

CHAPTER 9 **I HAVE WRITTEN MY WILL. NOW WHAT?** 83
Discussion with executor /personal representative 83
Storage 83
Keep will updated 83
Keep related documents updated 83
Revocation 84
What is a codicil? 84
Points to note in writing a codicil 84
Should a will be discussed with family? 85
Can a will be contested? 85

CHAPTER 10 **OTHER INSTRUMENTS FOR CONSIDERATION** 87
Life insurance 87
Trusts 88
Power of Attorney 90
Living Wills 91
Letter of Wishes 91

CHAPTER 11 **THE TIME IS NOW!** 93

APPENDICES

Appendix 1 Sample: Simple Will Form frequently used in Jamaica 97
Appendix 2 Sample: Florida Last Will And Testament Form 99
Appendix 3 Sample: Durable Financial Power Of Attorney 105
Appendix 4 Sample: Living Will 111
Appendix 5 Sample: Letter of Wishes 117
Appendix 6 Sample: Codicil to Will Form 119

1 WHY WRITE A WILL?

"All good men and women must take responsibility to create legacies that will take the next generation to a level we could only imagine."

Jim Rohn

WHAT IS A WILL?

A will is a legal document in which a person, known as a testator, voluntarily specifies how their assets (estate or things owned) pass after death. This document, in which assets transfer to beneficiaries, is expected to be honest, with non-fraudulent intention, written by an adult over eighteen years old, and is legally binding in a court of law. When writing the will, the testator should be competent, that is, of sound mind, acting without undue influence, and have the authority to transfer those assets. However, if there is proof that the testator signed under less ideal conditions, the will could be contested in the courts.

THE IMPORTANCE OF WRITING A WILL

The importance of writing a will cannot be overemphasized. People have the perfect opportunity to take care of their loved ones while they are alive, but what of the future? They would no doubt want to continue to support the people they love. A will sets out plans for the future care of loved ones and gives peace of mind that their affairs will be taken care of after death according to their wishes. Hopefully, this will prevent family rifts that are so common when a will is absent.

Most importantly, nobody knows when they will die. Rather than procrastinating or having negative thoughts about writing a will, they should prepare it on time. Some people learn the importance of having a will in place the hard way. Sometimes it is too late to get it done, as writing a will on one's deathbed might not allow enough time to ensure it meets all the legal requirements and family considerations.

Dying without leaving a valid will, termed ***dying intestate*** *(Chapter 5)*, gives up the right to decide on distributing one's assets to the beneficiaries of their choice. The absence of a will gives authority to the state to determine the distribution of one's estate and to pass the assets to the next of kin in an order specified by law, known as ***intestate succession***. Once living, the kin would inherit based on his position on the list. If one kin dies, the next one on the list will inherit, so those listed further down on the list might inherit nothing if others are still living.

Usually, the estate passes to the spouse and children. Sometimes, a surviving spouse would receive half of the estate, and if there are no children or grandchildren, they will receive the entire estate.

In some instances, the state passes the legacy of predeceased children to their children and grandchildren. The order of next of kin would typically be spouse, then children, parents, siblings, aunts and uncles, nieces and nephews, and cousins. Friends and charities would not be on the list prepared by the state. Some territories do not regard unmarried partners as next of kin, despite the closeness before death or the time they had been together and would receive nothing from the estate unless stated in a will.

Each territory has its own rules. Persons should seek legal advice on the regulations in their respective areas, but it is best to have a valid will to avoid the state having the power to allocate one's hard-earned assets.

Writing a will is crucial to protect one's family, and its importance cannot be overemphasized. It is the hope that its relevance will be highlighted between these pages to convince and provide enough motivation to get it done at the earliest. Some people procrastinate for years and never get it done.

What are some reasons for having a will? How can writing a will and organizing an estate be done in an organized, efficient, and cost-effective way?

Some reasons for writing a will:

- Protecting a family in the event the breadwinner predeceases them
- Reduce the chances of persons who feel they have the legal right to an estate contesting one's will
- Making provisions for the future care of children
- Ensuring one's death is less stressful for their survivors
- Maintaining the care of someone with a disability who might not be a relative
- Protecting an unmarried spouse from disinheritance and financial hardship
- Providing for a family from a previous relationship
- Continuing support for someone who is not a relative and currently receives financial support
- Contributing to a church, school, or a favorite charity
- Disinheriting heirs
- Saving on inheritance and estate taxes
- Leaving clear directives regarding a business
- Forgiving debtors
- Confirming plans to be an organ donor
- Leaving support for pets

Having identified some of the critical reasons to make a will, one has a choice to make, have a will and decide on the heirs to an estate, or have the state make that decision. The reasons above are discussed in more detail below:

PROTECTING FAMILY

Family protection is a significant consideration for several people. Creating a will is essential to ensure that the protection provided for one's family while they are alive will continue after their demise. The death of a loved one, especially of a breadwinner, can be stressful for family members. They need to take care of funeral arrangements and all that goes with it, and then they must deal with carrying on with their lives without their breadwinner. Adequate preparations made on their behalf make it easier and less stressful for them.

Families usually appreciate the kind gesture of a legacy left them by their breadwinners. They feel loved and appreciated knowing that thought went into preparing them for any eventuality. Making a will goes a long way in protecting families and easing their financial burden after a breadwinner's death. It makes it easier and less stressful for them to adjust to life and, as we say in the life insurance industry, "Your widow or widower would not have to marry the first 'meal ticket' that comes along."

PROTECTING ESTATES

Families own and use their assets, then pass them on to beneficiaries of their choice and future generations. Having a will in place is one sure way of protecting an estate and ensuring it passes to beneficiaries of one's choice. It can protect assets from creditors and save on taxes, among others.

PROTECTING MINOR CHILDREN

Parents love their children and do all that is necessary and possible for them while they are alive; they love and care for them and give them the best education, the best of everything they can afford. However, what happens when parents die? A parent can use a will to make provisions for the care of their children after death. Children under eighteen, ***minors***, cannot legally be beneficiaries unless there is a named guardian or trustee *(Chapter 3)* who would be given this authority in the will.

CARING FOR SOMEONE WITH SPECIAL NEEDS

Disability can be short-term or long-term and, in either case, can be costly. A provider can use a will to provide continued care for someone with a disability whom they assist. If the disabled person is not an immediate family member protected by the rules of intestacy, providing for this individual should be through a will.

PREPARING FOR AN UNMARRIED SPOUSE

Married spouses enjoy certain privileges, including legal and financial benefits, the right to inherit marital property, and the right to legal divorce proceedings, among others. However, the laws in different jurisdictions specify the definitions of marriage. Some recognize marriage only as those unions that receive a marriage certificate after a civil or religious ceremony. Others define even the genders of the spouses, some not recognizing same-sex marriages.

Unions, where spouses live together without a formal certificate, are common-law marriages. Some jurisdictions do not recognize common-law marriages, whereas some recognize them after living together as man and wife for a minimum number of years and identifying as spouses.

In the United States, a few states recognize common-law marriages, including Alabama, Colorado, Iowa, Kansas, Montana, New Hampshire (for inheritance only), Oklahoma, Rhode Island, South Carolina, Texas and Utah, and the District of Columbia. The 1868 Florida law made illegal the cohabitation between a man and a woman without being married. In April 2016, they repealed a section of the law and later abolished it in its entirety.

Before 1968, Florida recognized common-law marriages, but the current law dictates that "no common-law marriage entered into after January 1, 1968, shall be valid." Florida, therefore, still recognizes common-law marriages before January 1, 1968. The exception to this Florida law is that couples who were common-law married in one of the states that still recognize common-law marriages, even after January 1, 1968, are still recognized in Florida as being legally married. Florida was the 36th State to legalize same-sex marriages. Nonetheless, the law still states that a marriage is only between a woman and a man.

In areas where unmarried unions are not recognized, the local laws governing inheritances do not protect unmarried spouses. The deceased spouse's assets will not automatically be passed to the surviving partner but, instead, to other family members. Without a will stating that an asset will pass to the surviving partner, they could be traumatized emotionally and financially. In addressing the status of common-law marriages, the law also addresses the spouses' entitlements. For example, in Jamaica, the law recognizes common-law marriages if individuals live together as man and wife for over five years. Section 2 of The Property (Rights of Spouses) Act in Jamaica defines a spouse as "a single man and a single woman who have been cohabiting together as if they were, in law, husband and wife, for no less than five years; and for the purpose of succession, the partners must have been cohabiting for at least five years immediately before the death of one of the spouses."

Things could get complicated for a surviving common-law spouse in some territories from the examples above. Persons in common-law marriages should become aware of the laws governing these relationships in their respective regions. If so desired, they make their wills naming each other as their beneficiary to eliminate any complications that could otherwise result if one died intestate.

PLANNING FOR BLENDED FAMILIES

With the high divorce rate these days, blended families have become commonplace. On occasions, the new couple has left their legacy to each other and disinherited the children from a previous relationship. Parents with children from a prior relationship should ensure the protection of those children in the event of their death. Minor children brought in a new relationship may have the other parent sharing custody. Their legacy should be in a will with a named trustee, saving the added stress and confusion that sometimes result.

UNLISTED BENEFICIARIES

People at times get close to persons, causes, or organizations other than family members and elect to leave a legacy for them. They name these individuals or organizations in a will to prevent state intervention by intestate succession.

PROTECTING BUSINESSES

Without a proper succession plan for a business, it stands to fail. A will creates the opportunity for company equity to pass to the co-owners or other beneficiaries with a clear goal. Deciding on the recipients can be difficult, primarily if some family members worked in the business and some did not. A will allows the testator to state clear instructions for the continuation of the company or for properly winding it up.

SAVING ON INHERITANCE AND ESTATE TAXES

Tax evasion is illegal, but taxes can be legally avoided. Even after death, taxes are due to the state. A large portion of one's estate might pay these outstanding taxes, and another large chunk pays legal fees. An accountant will advise how to legally avoid taxes and provide guidance in structuring an estate to minimize taxes on cash and property.

The implementation of these tax-saving strategies can increase the payout to heirs. For example, in the United States, the law allows gift-giving to a maximum of US$15,000 per person per annum ($16,000 in 2022) without attracting a gift tax. This figure reduces the value of the estate, thus reducing the estate tax liability. A gift of $12,000 to each of five children calculated at $60,000 per annum multiplied by, say, five years would reduce the value of the estate by $300,000. There is no limit to the number of persons to whom one can give a gift, but there is a lifetime exemption of $11.7 million (Increased to $12.06 million in 2022).

An estate planner may also discuss the possibility of using trusts and early transfer of assets to beneficiaries. Although it might result in loss of control, to save on taxes, some assets may be given as gifts while one is alive, or establish trust funds. There is usually a threshold for the amount treated as tax-free. Your estate planner will discuss these tax-saving strategies.

CONTRIBUTING TO CHARITY

Persons may have spent many years contributing their time and money to their favorite charity and would like to leave a legacy for that charity after their death. They may even make a bequest to a charity they have never been associated. Creating this legacy would be best stated in a will, as the charity would not appear on the list for intestate succession without one.

Interestingly, contributions to a charity may be tax-free to the giver, subject to a limit, allowing for continuing the giver's legacy. If the charity of choice has several branches or is an international organization, the information should be in the will, making the distribution effortless.

In some US states, the testator's power to make charitable gifts is limited to a maximum percentage of the estate to protect the surviving family members from disinheritance. Some states prohibit deathbed gifts made to charities within a specified time before death. An estate planner or attorney in a territory can provide more information on this issue.

DISINHERITING HEIRS

DISINHERITING CHILDREN

An heir is a family member who stands to inherit from an estate after the owner's death. Dying intestate would position heirs to benefit from an estate based on the rules of intestacy. The intestacy laws differ by jurisdiction, but the law would allow an estate to be distributed to a spouse and children first in several states. In some cases, adopted children are regarded as heirs while stepchildren are not, so a will best dictates the distribution of assets.

Although some immediate family members might feel entitled to a legacy from an estate, most states allow the disinheritance of adult children. Some exceptions include protecting unborn children left off the will. Children with disabilities are also covered.

In Louisiana, disabled children under the age of twenty-four may inherit a quarter or a half of the parent's estate. One should note the intention to disinherit a child or children in a will to prevent contest in court on the grounds of oversight.

A will may include a disinherited heir with a minimal inheritance, for example, one dollar, stating that the omitted heir is intentional. He may also be named on the will with clear instructions to receive nothing. Usually, one does not have to mention a reason for disinheritance, but in Louisiana, one must state a legally acceptable reason.

DISINHERITING A SPOUSE

Marriage gives a spouse the legal right to inherit property from a deceased spouse whether or not the deceased left a will. Surviving married spouses, in some states, are protected in the event of intestacy. If a spouse receives nothing from a will, they can request to take a portion of the estate. The state decides on the percentage based on the number of years they were married. Some states do not offer this protection. Their provision covers the period of the marriage, making only property acquired by one spouse during the marriage become the property of both spouses.

Florida law protects surviving spouses and some surviving children from total disinheritance. If the decedent had remarried or had children after writing the last will and not mentioned them in the will, they are entitled to a share of the estate. An attorney best handles the statutory rights of the applicable laws.

FORGIVING DEBTS

The forgiveness of a debtor or debtors must be stated in a will because the state will not make this allowance in an intestate estate.

DONATING ORGANS

Persons considering organ donation or preferences regarding life support should discuss their wishes beforehand, as decisions might become necessary before the probate of the will. Another consideration might be a Living Will. *(Chapter 10).*

CARING FOR PETS

Pet lovers cover their pets with reimbursement insurance for accidents and illnesses but might consider ensuring their pets are cared for after death. They should include their desire in their will and name the person who would care for the pet. Never leave assets in the name of pets.

ETCHED IN MY MEMORY

Preparing for an unmarried spouse

John and Jane lived together in Florida in a common-law relationship for four years. Florida does not recognize their union, so when John died without leaving a will, Jane was not entitled to any part of his estate.

Planning for blended families

Kingsley and Althea were married for twelve years. Together they had three children and later got divorced. Kingsley then married Jennifer, and together they had two children.

Kingsley left a will that included his children from his marriage to Althea. It saved the time, pain, and agony for Althea to battle with Jennifer for her children to benefit legally from his estate.

Disinheriting children

Two individuals disinherited their adult children because they did not like their spouse or sexual orientation. They specifically named them in their wills, with a token legacy of one dollar, which was deemed not to have been an oversight.

In Florida, as in Jamaica, a parent is under no obligation to leave a legacy for their adult children, but they would have to state their wishes in their will. Once there is no will, the law of intestacy allows each child to receive their percentage of the estate.

A will solves any uncertainty.

Disinheriting a spouse

Vivid is my memory of a childhood neighbor, Mr. Brown, who died during my tenure in life insurance in Jamaica. In his will, he tried to disinherit his wife by naming her with a token legacy.

They had six grown children, and she was a full-time homemaker and mother to all their children. He died while they were still married, and, in his will, he instructed that she should receive only one chair.

Thankfully, she contested it and received her share of the estate.

2 WHAT CONSTITUTES A VALID WILL?

"The things you do for yourself are gone when you are gone, but the things you do for others remain as your legacy."

N. D. Kalu

TYPES OF WILLS

JOINT WILLS

In a joint will, a couple decides on the death of one partner to leave all their assets to the surviving partner. On the death of that surviving partner, the remaining assets are to pass to the couple's named beneficiaries. Joint wills are less frequently used as they cannot be revoked once one partner dies.

LIVING WILLS

A Living Will gives instructions about medical treatment and life-saving measures when one cannot communicate his wishes. *(Chapter 10).*

FORMATS OF A WILL

TYPEWRITTEN WILLS

A testator uses a simple will to give instructions for distributing his assets to his beneficiaries in an uncomplicated estate. A will provides a permanent record of instructions for distributing an estate and is usually typed. Although there may be other ways to prepare a will, a typed version gives fewer possibilities for a contest. In some instances, a testator may make a handwritten (holographic) or an oral/spoken (nuncupative) will, but some territories do not recognize them. One should always check to find out what is legal in their respective area, but the safest bet is to make a typewritten will. A sample of a simple will is in *Appendix 1.*

HANDWRITTEN WILLS

Most states do not recognize handwritten or holographic wills - those written and signed in the testator's handwriting, and the states that recognize them have set rules for their execution.

SPOKEN OR ORAL WILLS

Someone makes an oral (nuncupative) will, referred to as the deathbed will, when they become suddenly ill, are in extreme danger, death is imminent, and there is no opportunity to prepare a written will.

An oral will constitutes an individual calling two or more persons to listen to and serve as witnesses to their wishes. This type of will presents opportunities for fraud and is not widely accepted as it might be challenging to prove the validity and could cause disagreements among surviving family members. States that accept oral wills place specific stipulations on them for legal consideration. Some, for example, might specify the need for proof that an individual made the will in anticipation of imminent death, meaning it would be difficult to prove there was an oral will and that it was made within the allowed number of hours before the death of the testator.

Sometimes oral wills are accepted for distributing personal property but not real property. Exceptions are made in some areas of the United States for soldiers and sailors while on active military duty or at sea, allowing for holographic or nuncupative wills to pass personal and real property to their beneficiaries. Some states have added stipulations to include a limited accepted period after the testator leaves the service. While some do not have this stipulation, they allow passing personal and real property in nuncupative wills.

STIPULATIONS OF A VALID WILL

MENTAL CAPACITY OF THE TESTATOR

The testator must be mentally competent at the time of writing his will. He is considered mentally incompetent if he has a mental deficiency, is intoxicated, or is under the influence of drugs when writing his will.

TESTAMENTARY CAPACITY AND INTENT

A testator possessing testamentary capacity is over eighteen and is aware that he is distributing his assets to beneficiaries in a will. It should also be clear that the contents of the will are the intended wishes of the testator.

FREE OF UNDUE INFLUENCE

The testator should not be writing his will under any undue circumstances, fraud, or duress. If any of these conditions exist, his wishes will not be acknowledged but declared null and void.

TIME AND PLACE

A will needs to be signed and dated simultaneously by the testator in the presence of at least two witnesses. If, for example, a testator writes his will on his hospital bed and he can see the witnesses in the distance, the will is considered valid upon the signing by the witnesses. If, however, the will is taken to the witnesses in a place where the testator cannot see them, it would not be considered valid.

ETCHED IN MY MEMORY

A Texas, United States case

Oral Will

In a Texas case, McClain vs. Adams 1941, when she thought she was at the point of death, a woman called someone to her bedside on a Thursday to leave her property to a friend. She felt well enough to visit a neighbor by Saturday and then went to the grocery store before dying later that night.

The court ruled that she was not at the point of death when she made her oral will, had enough time to have prepared a written will before she died, and declared the will null and void.

3 CONTENTS OF A WILL

"A good man leaveth an inheritance to his children's children: and the wealth of the sinner is laid up for the just."

Proverbs 13:22

PARTIES TO A WILL

TESTATOR

The testator is the person who makes the will and decides on how his assets are distributed. It is after his death that the will is probated and his wishes carried out.

EXECUTOR

In the will, the testator names an executor or executrix (personal representative in the United States) responsible for carrying out the instructions in the will. He may also give this responsibility to more than one person or an organization.

BENEFICIARY

A beneficiary is a person who will inherit from an estate in the manner stipulated by a will.

GUARDIAN

The person named in a will to take care of the testator's minor children (under age eighteen) is the guardian, and they may also be the trustee.

TRUSTEE

A trustee is a person or organization responsible for the financial decisions of minor children until they reach the age of majority. The testator may list an alternative if the first selected trustee refuses or cannot act.

WITNESSES

There should be two witnesses to the testator's signature on the will. Witnesses do not need to read the will; they sign as witnesses to the testator's signature.

CHECKLIST FOR CONSIDERATION IN WRITING A WILL

The checklist for writing a will is quite simple. The laws covering some of the topics differ from region to region. It would be helpful to find out the rules of law pertaining to the relevant issues in an area.

EXECUTOR

In this demanding and time-consuming role, an executor administers an estate, carries out the testator's wishes, and distributes the assets to the beneficiaries.

The role includes filing the probate, paying all outstanding debts and taxes, notifying the death to all institutions with which the deceased had a relationship, for example, banks and social security; collecting from debtors; and maintaining the property until it is sold or passed to the beneficiaries.

The executor might need to appear in court on behalf of the decedent, act as trustee for minor children, or, if the testator was an organ donor, deliver the organ on time, to the correct place, and in proper condition. Some organs need to be delivered within hours and others up to the first twenty-four hours after death, after which they become unusable. Their role could also include being the trustee or guardian for minor children.

The executor qualifies by law for a percentage of the estate as payment (find out the rate in your area), but they may decide whether to accept that payment. The executor may also be a beneficiary, so a testator may consider appointing a beneficiary as the executor since that person has a vested interest in the estate. For these critical reasons, the testator should discuss this charge with the intended executor or executors and allow them to accept or refuse the responsibility.

The testator should list an alternative in case the first selected executor refuses or cannot act. If a will is sizable and complex, it might be in the best interest of the testator to consider a bank or trust company as executor to administer their estate as they bring technical and legal expertise and experience to the job.

Some states decide on the eligibility of the named person or persons to act as personal representatives and whether an out-of-state person can serve. Eligibility considerations include being at least eighteen years of age, physically and mentally capable of performing the assigned duties, and not being convicted of a felony. In some states, for example, Florida, the personal representative must also be a state resident.

The Jamaica Wills Act stipulates that "at least one executor, but no more than four, whom the testator trusts must be appointed under the will, so that person will act with alacrity and take on duties of executorship and administer the estate in a quick time, or very soon after the death of the testator." However, the testator should appoint at least two executors. If one dies, will not, or cannot serve, another will be available to carry out the duties.

In some US states, the law requires that the executor be a family member, such as a spouse, sibling, parent, or child, but generally, a testator may choose his executor outside this group.

An executor needs to be carefully selected. Thought should be given to several factors:

- Is this person responsible?
- Will they carry out the task professionally after the testator's death?

Too frequently, testators appoint executors without their knowledge and then file away the will, leading to confusion at death. They should point out to the executor any exceptional situations and how to handle them, including items like special needs for children who might not be able to take care of themselves at the age of majority, special wishes for a business, or pets. They should ensure that one's family has the contact information for the executor and that the executor has a copy of the will. Along with the will, they should store the contact information for the accountants, financial planners, trust companies, and any other individual or business employed to prepare the will. Without a will, an administrator named by the state performs all the responsibility.

BENEFICIARIES

In several jurisdictions, marriage automatically revokes a will, so if written before marriage, or if the testator remarries, it becomes his responsibility to write a new will after marriage.

In Jamaica, the surviving spouse of a common-law marriage will need a declaration from the court stating that they are the deceased's spouse. A spouse is entitled to all personal chattels, including, among other things, motor vehicles, jewelry, paintings, and furniture of the deceased partner unless they were in use for business purposes. They are also entitled to 10% of the net estate with interest of 10% until paid.

Through a will, a testator in Florida may exercise succession planning for his family, his business, and any other interests. His personal representative or administrator will be responsible for transferring his possessions to his beneficiaries. An unmarried partner could benefit as a beneficiary on a will but does not stand to gain on an estate if there is no will.

GUARDIAN

Parents should have a named guardian responsible for taking care of their children. They must carefully think through this decision to make the best selection for them. This decision should not be taken lightly and need to be in a will to prevent the court from having to make decisions on the children's welfare.

Some points to be considered in selecting a guardian include:

- Can this person be trusted to care for the children?
- Will they make the right decisions regarding the children's health, education, and financial needs?
- Do they already have a bond with the children?
- Does this person share a comparable lifestyle?
- Do they have similar values?
- Does this person have similar religious beliefs?
- Do they have children or plan to have children?

If the prospective guardian and trustee is someone other than a spouse, this person should give their consent to taking on this responsibility. This request for their approval prepares them and allows them to refuse if so desired.

Parents should also discuss the selection of the guardian for their minors and include it in both their wills. If they die simultaneously, there would be no confusion regarding the guardian. Naming a second guardian helps if the first choice cannot serve at one's death.

TRUSTEE

The trustee will handle the financial aspect of the minor children's lives until they are of the age of majority (18 or 21, depending on the jurisdiction). In the case of a child with special needs, this responsibility might go into adulthood.

The same person can be the guardian and the trustee but choosing different people to perform the roles would make for more discussion and collaboration toward the welfare of the children.

The testator may wish to establish a trust *(Chapter 10)* while alive or put it in his will, instructing his executor to implement it after his death. Using a recognized financial institution as the trustee is an option.

When leaving a minor as a beneficiary on a life insurance policy or retirement account, the owner also names a trustee on the account. The trustee is responsible for managing the finances in the child's interest until the age of majority.

GIFTS TO MINORS UNDER FLORIDA LAW

The Uniform Transfers to Minors Act allows gifts left to minors without the establishment of a Trust, to be managed by custodians until the minor reaches the age of majority. Each state has its version of this law. If one gifts a child under the Uniform Transfers to Minors Act in his state and leaves proceeds from a life insurance policy or retirement account without a named trustee, the court will appoint a trustee to manage the gift until the child is eighteen. The money is placed in a custodial account for the child's benefit to a certain age. If the terms of the trust dictate the management of the funds to the child attaining a specific age, say twenty-one (21), the trustee would be responsible for managing the funds to that age, after which it terminates, and the "child" would then become responsible for managing the funds.

In Florida, the law provides different scenarios where a child may inherit a legacy. In establishing a trust for minor children, the trustee must get a tax identification number, open a bank account in the name of the trust using the tax identification number, and distribute the assets based on the instructions given in the trust. The trustee keeps accurate records, files annual tax returns, communicates with the child and ensures the responsible spending of the money.

Under the Act, each state sets a time limit to the agreement. The giver must specify in his gift the age at which the arrangement will terminate, for example, "I gift $15,000 to Jane Brown, as custodian for her son, John Brown, under the Uniform Transfers to Minors Act, to age 18."

The Florida Uniform Transfers to Minors Act stipulates that the arrangement must end before the minor reaches age 21.

GIFTS TO MINORS IN JAMAICA

In Jamaica, when transferring assets to minors through a will, a trustee must be appointed to give oversight until the minor reaches the age of majority, age eighteen (18).

With intestacy, the Administrator-General's Act mandates that the Administrator-General administers the estate until the last minor turns 18. If anyone else wishes to administer an intestate estate, they must apply through a court order.

ASSETS AND LIABILITIES

Assets are all the things we own, and liabilities are all the things we owe. To prepare for writing a will, a list of all our assets and liabilities is essential.

LIABILITIES

Liabilities include all debts – personal taxes, property taxes, estate duties, business and personal loans, credit card debts, mortgages, equity loans, car loans, student loans, personal loans, outstanding medical bills, funeral expenses, and other bills.

It is essential to have enough in an estate to cover debts as an executor must pay all liabilities before any portion of an estate can be assigned to beneficiaries. There are ways of addressing a shortfall in an estate.

ASSETS

Assets may include real estate, motor vehicles, bank accounts, stocks and bonds, investment accounts, retirement accounts, business and business interests, life insurance policies, and other valuable personal property like artwork, musical instruments, firearm collections, antiques, jewelry, and heirlooms.

Some assets can be valued, but others have more emotional or sentimental value, including cherished items that would preferably be kept in the family.

Receivables are an asset to the estate. Questions for the testator to ponder would include, Are there debtors? Is there a plan to forgive any debtors? Shall all assets be passed to heirs? Should the executor collect the debts or liquidate some assets to add cash to the estate? Early planning and putting one's wishes in a will make the executive's job easier.

The remaining balance between the assets and the liabilities, the ***residuary estate***, is distributed to the beneficiaries.

OTHER ELEMENTS TO CONSIDER

LIFE INSURANCE

Life insurance adds value to an estate to help ensure the testator's wishes can be covered. *(Chapter 10).*

BANK ACCOUNTS

- ***Bank Accounts with a sole owner***
  Cash from bank accounts with sole owners will go through probate and pass to the beneficiary or beneficiaries named in the will. Without a will, the account goes through the laws of intestacy. In some US states, dependent on the size of the account, the beneficiaries may present a sworn statement, a death certificate, and proof of their identity to the bank indicating that they are entitled to the money.
- ***Accounts with a Payable-on-Death Beneficiary***
  A "payable-on-death beneficiary" on a bank account quickly receives funds without probate. The account holder completes a form supplied by the bank. The payable-on-death beneficiary can claim the money with a death certificate and identification upon the account holder's death. The named beneficiary is not entitled to any funds while the account holder is alive.
- ***Joint Accounts***
  A joint bank account avoids probate and delays transferring money to the joint account holder. On the death of a joint account holder, the funds pass to the other without probate.

  Sometimes, however, joint accounts carry the "right of survivorship," which states that the money passes to the survivor on the death of the joint account holder. This information is relevant, especially if an individual opens an account and later adds another account holder. This addition may be for convenience; for example, one might name a joint account holder to give easy access to transact business on their behalf or cover funeral expenses without the intention of all the money passing to this individual on his death.

  The account holder's intentions must be clear to the bank to avoid confusion after death, as legally, without clear instructions, this additional account holder will be entitled to the money on the original account holder's death. Optionally, one might open a separate smaller joint account with just enough to cover specific transactions and give the additional account holder full access.

PROPERTY OWNERSHIP

A significant asset would probably be property ownership. In considering the distribution of property to beneficiaries, the testator must consider whether they own the property in joint tenancy or tenancy in common, as this affects the treatment in writing a will.

- ***Property owned by joint tenancy***
  Assets owned by joint tenancy stipulate that full ownership of the asset passes to the surviving owner on the death of one of the owners without a will. Therefore, a joint owner cannot leave an asset owned by joint tenancy to a beneficiary until after the death of the joint partner. The asset, however, may be mentioned in a will with a named potential beneficiary and a clause indicating that it will become effective only if the testator survives the joint owner. However, if the surviving owner dies without naming a beneficiary, or if both owners die simultaneously, the asset falls under the law of intestacy.
- ***Property owned by tenancy in common***
  Properties owned by tenancy in common are owned by more than one individual, each holding a specific percentage of the property. On the death of one owner, the applicable portion of the asset passes to the estate of the deceased, or to their beneficiaries. In an intestate estate, their portion falls under the laws of intestacy.
- ***Foreign property***
  An estate planner or attorney should prepare the will for an estate that includes foreign property. They need to be advised of all the details regarding foreign properties to best assist them in giving advice. The law may require a separate will for each country. There are instances where the law in one state or country may dictate heirship, preventing the owner from selecting a beneficiary.

  The testator should inform the executor of all foreign properties and the names and contacts of any estate planner/legal advisor with whom the property owner may have dealt.

TYPES OF TRANSFERS OF PROPERTY

Property transfer can be inter vivos (while alive) or mortis causa (after death). The implications should be understood. The rates of taxation are covered later. *(Chapter 4)*.

Inter Vivos Transfers

Inter vivos transfers may be through sale to increase cash into an estate or by gifting to a beneficiary while one is alive. Inter vivos transfers cause the owner to lose control of the property but pass the attendant taxes to the beneficiary. The transfer reduces the owner's assets and the related taxes.

Mortis Causa Transfers

In Mortis Causa transfers, the owner maintains ownership and control of the property while alive and pays taxes until death. The executor then carries out the terms of the will and transfers the property to the named beneficiary, who will become liable for future taxes on the property.

OTHER ASSETS

The world is constantly changing, and especially with the onset of the internet and technological developments, some assets are often overlooked. People tend to spend much time online without realizing that some of their actions may be accumulating assets for them, yet they may not focus on them in that light. Daily online activities include subscriptions, bill payments, auto-renewal, online banking, online businesses, streamed videos and movies, blogging, businesses, book clubs, and shopping.

Many online transactions can have implications for an individual. Some might be assets and others liabilities. What happens to them on the death of that individual? Online transactions that are assets need to be accounted for and willed to beneficiaries because, without this, sometimes, not even a personal representative will have access to some online accounts.

- ***Digital assets***

  The definition of digital assets changes as fast as the offerings on the internet increase. Initially, digital assets referred to photos, videos and files. With such an explosion in online activities, the definition has broadened to include all records owned or which can be stored and accessed digitally. These would consist of email, social media accounts, online businesses, online banking, cloud storage, blogs, and other accounts requiring a login.

  For businesses, the definition expands to include valuable resources to the company. These encompass logos, pictures, graphics, audio files, videos, animations, presentations, business websites, domain names, blogs, business processes, applications, business inventory, intellectual property, online marketing material, design files, and business documents. Businesses use and store vast amounts of data daily and should consider investing in a digital asset management system to meticulously organize, store and allow controlled access to the data. This will also integrate their systems to allow for efficiency, a better customer experience, and growth.

LIST ALL DIGITAL ASSETS

The internet has changed the world as we know it. Digital assets now need to be considered for inclusion among other assets and included in wills. They are thought of in a new way today. One needs to start listing their digital assets and keep the list updated with each new additional transaction.

What are some of the digital assets that might be overlooked? These should be included in a will.

- Marketplace accounts like Amazon, Etsy, and eBay
- Payment accounts like PayPal, CashApp, and Western Union
- Information stored in the cloud
- Information in Dropbox accounts
- Contact lists or databases
- Credit card cashback programs
- Frequent Flyer miles and other Rewards Programs
- Online businesses
- Domain names
- Social media income-generating accounts

Many of these transactions have earning potential, and owners should include them in their estates and wills. An executor will need access to the testator's online businesses, online sales accounts, payment platforms, current orders for delivery, and the ability to stop future sales and make refunds on incomplete sales.

OTHER DIGITAL ACTIVITIES

An executor could be exposed to an allegation of waste if the assets become insufficient to pay all the estate debts. Unless all activities are made known to the executor, it might be challenging to ascertain them. To make it easier for the executor, the testator should include the numbers and passwords for bank accounts, credit card accounts, safety deposit box numbers and passwords, and permission to access and terminate those accounts.

It becomes problematic when someone with a fiduciary relationship to the deceased, like an executor, does not have access to accounts, especially if they have a monetary value. When the service provider denies the executor access, they are, in essence, blocking them from carrying out the provisions of the will.

Some service providers argue that their users do not own their accounts but only the content, and allowing access would violate the terms of service between them and the user and would breach their privacy rights. In the United States, The Uniform Fiduciary Access to Digital Assets Act (2015) recommended full access to accounts owned by the decedent. However, the individual's privacy came into question, and the Revised Uniform Fiduciary Access to Digital Assets Act of 2015 now protects the individual's privacy and gives limited access to the individual's personal representative. Some US states have enacted this law, some with alterations, granting the executor access to the online accounts owned by the deceased. Florida, for example, adopted it through its Florida Fiduciary Access to Digital Assets Act of 2016. Sometimes, the executor must provide evidence linking the account to the principal and prove to the judge how the information will help probate the will.

Some argue that the Internal Revenue Services (IRS) agents can search the internet and identify taxpayers' online activities, including their social media profiles, e-commerce activities, websites, and domain names. They can value domain sales, marketability, keyword search popularity, and search frequency. Therefore, it is wise to declare all of one's assets, including digital assets.

Today, with the advances in reproductive technology, additional digital assets to be considered are eggs frozen by many women for their future use. This could create a challenge in estate planning as persons are unsure whether to include possible descendants from those eggs. It is further complicated if frozen eggs are donated to others who cannot conceive. The trendsetters like Apple, Facebook, and Google offer the cost of freezing their eggs for future use as a company benefit to single women. There is no telling how many other companies might adopt this trend. One must decide whether to include frozen eggs in her will as it might affect future generations. A discussion with an estate planner will guide the testator in wording her will to include this asset if she so desires.

It becomes evident that digital assets are a part of probate inventory and estate tax returns. One does not have to give full access to their online activities, and they do have the right to protect their privacy. They can decide how much access to give their fiduciary to act on their behalf, but others must know their decision. Much more will develop on this topic as it evolves.

- ***Social Media Pages and Email***
  Personal and business emails are other significant items for privacy level consideration, but whatever the decision, it needs to be in a will. Many friends and family members manage active social media pages for their deceased loved ones. Some people argue that they would like their social media pages deactivated after death. Some would prefer them kept active so their children and grandchildren can look back and better understand their personalities and what they stood for. Some would like it maintained so friends can post memoirs on their special days. Something worth considering: If the choice is for an account to be kept active, instructions could be left for "The late" or "Fond memories of" in front of the name, so new visitors to the managed page know the status. Facebook offers the opportunity for users to record their preferences and the names of the selected persons to control the page, if desired.

VIDEO WILLS

We are fully experiencing the digital age, and some people have started putting their wills on video. At the time of writing, these wills are not legally enforceable by themselves, as a will still has to be written, signed, witnessed, and in some cases, notarized.

However, video wills could serve a useful purpose. They can demonstrate that the testator fulfilled the stipulations of a valid will, showing they possessed the mental and testamentary capacity, acted on their free will, and were not under undue influence. It could even capture the signing of the will.

A video will could possibly be used in place of a letter of wishes *(Chapter 10/Appendix 5)* to record reasons for decisions a person may have made in their will, and which they feel might warrant an explanation to prevent family conflict.

A lawyer will offer advise on the current laws regarding video wills in your area.

VALUE THE ASSETS

Now that the physical, financial, and digital assets are listed, the testator should extend an approximate value beside each item to guide them in allocating the assets.

NAMING THE BENEFICIARIES

Now it is decision-making time! The testator needs to list all of their beneficiaries. The list should detail all assets, liabilities, and the already assigned assets and named beneficiaries. This will serve as a reminder when writing the will so that no one is overlooked except by design.

Deciding on the legacy for each beneficiary might take some careful thought. To be fair to one's family, a testator may consider their individual needs, the prospect of each taking care of himself, a child's unique needs, the contribution and support given by a child or children above the others, or if one worked in the family business. They may want to provide for an ex-spouse and children from a previous relationship or marriage.

The testator should provide the names and contacts of the beneficiaries for the executor.

For instances where a testator feels strongly about their decisions and thinks that some family members might feel unfairly treated, a Letter of Wishes *(Chapter 10 / Appendix 5)* may provide some explanation. This could also serve as evidence in a contested will.

WHAT SHOULD BE INCLUDED IN A WILL

Named in the will should be the executor, guardian, trustee for minor children, beneficiaries, and one's wishes for distributing residuary assets to beneficiaries.

ASSETS NOT ALREADY GIFTED

These include the assets and properties not already gifted to beneficiaries via instruments requiring named beneficiaries, such as a life insurance policy with a named beneficiary.

PROPERTIES OWNED BY TENANCY IN COMMON

Properties owned by tenancy in common entitles each owner to a percentage share of the property. Therefore, the testator is free to list their portion as part of their estate and pass it to their selected beneficiary.

RESIDUARY CLAUSE

A residuary clause is a statement in the will that serves as a capture for any assets not explicitly named therein. Maybe they were acquired after making the will, were forgotten, underestimated, or overlooked. It also includes assets and bequests that become void because a named beneficiary predeceased the testator and the will was not updated. The residuary estate must have a named beneficiary or beneficiaries. The residuary clause is of particular importance because, without it, any such assets would be treated separately by the court under the laws of intestacy.

An example of a residuary clause could be:

"All the rest and residue of my estate, I bequeath to........."

REVOCATION OF PREVIOUS WILLS AND CODICILS

At the start of a will, one needs to revoke all former wills or amendments to the will.

Examples of revocation of former wills:

Sample 1

I______________________________ of ____________________________ declare this to be my last will and testament. I hereby revoke all previous wills and codicils...

Sample 2

I______________________________ of ____________________________ revoke my former wills and codicils and declare this to be my last will and testament.

Sample 3

I______________________________ of ____________________________, being of competent and sound mind, do hereby declare this to be my last will and testament and do hereby revoke any and all wills and codicils heretofore made jointly or severally by me. I further declare that this Last Will & Testament reflects my personal wishes without any undue influence whatsoever.

WHAT SHOULD NOT BE INCLUDED IN A WILL

ASSETS THAT ARE ALREADY GIFTED

At the time of purchase or negotiation, some instruments require named beneficiaries. These include life insurance policies, trusts, stocks, bonds, pension benefits, social security, trusts, and annuities. With named beneficiaries, these assets would not fall within the ambit of the will, but instead the proceeds would be paid directly to the named beneficiaries after the owner's death. For this reason, these assets should not be included in a will.

PROPERTIES OWNED BY JOINT TENANCY

A property owned by joint tenancy also falls outside the ambit of the will. It passes to the surviving partner on the death of the joint owner. As recommended previously, a testator might wish to mention the property in his will, state that it is jointly owned, and that ownership passes on the death of the joint partner. The testator may appoint a potential beneficiary if his joint partner predeceases him and ownership of the property passes back to him.

JOINT BANK ACCOUNTS

As discussed earlier, joint bank accounts are owned by the account holders equally unless otherwise stated and will not be frozen by the bank on the death of one individual. These should not be included in a will.

FUNERAL PREFERENCES

Probating a will sometimes takes a long time. Since a will might be read and probated long after the funeral, a different medium should be used to express funeral preferences. Some people prefer to include these preferences

in their wills, and discuss them with their families and executors to ensure their wishes are honored.
The testator might want to include decisions on any of the following:

- Would they want to be cremated or buried?
- For a burial, is there a place of choice?
- Would they want a ceremony?
- Would they want a particular program at their funeral? Are there specific songs or hymns they would like included in the program?

Once there are preferences, they should be made known.

From a financial standpoint, preparations should be made for funeral arrangements and other urgent needs so the funds will be available before the will is probated. Depending on the preferred type of funeral, the individual's culture, and the burial cost, the testator might consider the expenses to cover a ceremony and a repast. There are ways to prepare for final expenses discussed in *Chapter 10.*

A DESIRE TO BE AN ORGAN DONOR

If there is a desire to be an organ donor, that wish would need to be made known to the family before death, including the relevant persons or organizations that will receive the organs. Since this is time-sensitive, the considered decision should be made known via a Living Will. *(Chapter 10).*

PUTTING CONDITIONS ON GIFTS

Gifts bequeathed to beneficiaries should not have conditions attached to them, for example, tying the receipt of a legacy to an accomplishment by a child. ("I bequeath one million dollars to my son, John, if he keeps the family business profitable.")

LEAVING PROPERTY FOR YOUR PET

If so desired, one should plan for the care of their pet by leaving funds in a will or a trust with the named caregiver as the beneficiary.

COMPLETION OF THE WILL

WHO SIGNS A WILL?

A will is signed and dated by the testator and two witnesses in the presence of each other. The witnesses do not need to read the will, their responsibility is only to witness the testator's signature. In most cases, the signature of a notary public or a justice of the peace is not essential for a will to be legally binding.

A self-proving affidavit is a sworn statement signed by the testator and two witnesses indicating that they have, under oath, signed and witnessed the will in the presence of the notary public. Florida wills include a self-proving affidavit and must be notarized. A self-proving affidavit may or may not be included in most other states. Once included, it must be notarized.

DATING A WILL

The testator and the two witnesses who sign the will must also date it at the same place, with the same date. Witnesses are required to indicate their addresses, although, at times, they use the address of the attorney's office.

4 DEATH DUTIES/ESTATE TAXES

"Legacy is not what I did for myself. It's what I'm doing for the next generation."

Vitor Belfort

It was Benjamin Franklin who, in 1789, wrote, "...in this world nothing can be said to be certain, except death and taxes." We now know that even in death, taxes are due. Some people argue that it is "more expensive to die."

A government imposes death duties on the assets of a deceased person. These taxes include estate taxes levied on the estate, paid out of the deceased's assets, and inheritance tax levied on the heirs to the estate.

Considering that taxes can be a high cost to an estate and are paid before the heirs can benefit, they should always be considered during the estate planning process. It is wise to research the tax laws in a particular territory, as they differ by jurisdiction. The findings will help in discussion with an attorney or estate planner.

DEATH TAXES IN FLORIDA

The personal representative or executor needs to pay taxes before creditors or beneficiaries. They might be held personally liable for a shortfall in taxes if they paid creditors and beneficiaries before paying the taxes. The maximum charge would be the amount paid to those creditors and beneficiaries.

The deceased is a separate taxpayer from the estate or trust, and each must receive its tax identification number to file its tax returns. A personal representative may apply for the nine-digit tax identification number for an estate, termed an employer identification number (EIN), used to open an account for the estate in the deceased's name. Online Internal Revenue Services (IRS) applications receive immediate responses, and those mailed on Form SS-4 receive answers in days. Applicants may download Form SS-4 and applications at the IRS.GOV website.

STATE AND FEDERAL INCOME TAX

Florida law exempts its residents from a state income tax and estate tax. Retirees are attracted to the state as they benefit from tax savings on Social Security benefits, IRA distributions, and other pension benefits. The residents, however, are not exempt from federal income tax.

The law does not count inherited property as income for federal income tax purposes. Coupled with Florida not imposing income tax, the heir does not accrue this tax.

FEDERAL ESTATE TAXES

Although the heirs to property are not taxed on their inheritance, the deceased's estate is levied with federal estate taxes on any property valued over a legal amount, indexed to inflation, and determined by the Government. Any estate valued under that figure would be exempt from federal estate taxes. In 2018 the threshold was US$5 million, raised to US$5,450,000, then US$11.18 million, then US$11.4 million in 2019 and US$11.58 in 2020, US$ 11.7million in 2021, and US$12.06 million in 2022 (double the amounts for married couples). With federal estate tax levied on estates over the existing threshold, the estimate of Americans who will pay this tax is only 11%.

A forty percent tax (40%) becomes due on properties valued over this nontaxable value. The executor must pay the federal estate tax for the estate in cash. Sometimes, executors need to liquidate assets to pay the tax. The decision can cause problems for valuable estates with predominantly illiquid assets like land. An attorney or estate planner will advise on the path to paying tax obligations.

INHERITANCE TAX

An inheritance tax is payable by a beneficiary, not an estate, on specific inherited assets. In Florida, however, the beneficiary pays no state income tax, estate tax, or inheritance tax on inheritance. The estates of Florida residents are administered in Florida under Florida law and are not subject to inheritance or state estate tax regardless of where the heirs live. Six states levy an inheritance tax: Iowa, Kentucky, Maryland, Nebraska, New Jersey, and Pennsylvania. Fifteen states (plus the District of Columbia) levy an estate tax: Connecticut, Delaware, Hawaii, Illinois, Maine, Maryland, Massachusetts, Minnesota, New Jersey, New York, Oregon, Rhode Island, Tennessee, Vermont, and Washington. Someone living in Florida who inherits property from someone living in one of the former six states might have to pay inheritance tax on their inheritance unless they were married to the deceased.

CAPITAL GAINS TAX

Tax basis is the difference between the purchase price and the selling price. Capital gains tax of 15% (23.8% for high earners) is levied on the tax basis. As an example, property bought at $150,000 and sold at $250,000 will attract 15% Capital Gains Tax on $100,000 that is, $15,000. Tax on property transferred to a beneficiary is calculated based on the difference between the value at death and the sales price, if higher, at a maximum of twenty percent (20%). Stocks and bonds also attract Capital Gains Tax on the increase in sales price over the valuation at the testator's death. Transfers to married spouses are exempt from capital gains tax.

DEATH DUTIES IN JAMAICA

Significant changes made to the tax laws in Jamaica in 2011 reflect a reduction in estate taxes. Up to June 2005, inter vivos transfers of property were at the rate of 7.5%, and mortis causa transfers at the rate of 15% of the property's value. In 2011 mortis causa tax rate was reduced to 1.5%. On March 7, 2019, the government announced a further tax reduction, implemented on April 1, 2019. Before this change, only estates valued under J$100,000 were exempt from transfer taxes. The new law raised the threshold to J$10 million, with the tax rate remaining at 1.5% of the property's value.

Properties owned as joint tenancy is charged tax only on the interest held in that property (usually 50%) by the testator on the death of one of the joint owners.

INHERITANCE TAX

There is no inheritance tax on properties in Jamaica.

CAPITAL GAINS TAX

Jamaica does not impose a capital gains tax. However, stamp duty becomes payable at property transfer and transfer tax on the asset's market value.

STAMP DUTY

Stamp duty in Jamaica is charged under the Stamp Duty Act. Unlike transfer tax, it is calculated on the assets that one owns, for example, land, shares, real estate not jointly owned, debentures, household contents, motor vehicles, life insurance policies with named beneficiaries, jewelry, and bank accounts. Before 2011, stamp duty was 3% of the estate's total value. As of April 1, 2019, stamp duty was reduced to a flat fee between J$5,000 to a maximum of J$25,000 (approximately US$166). This is based on the net estate value as follows:

Value of Estate	Stamp Duty
Under J$500,000	J$100 (Less than US$0.70)
J$10 million or less	J$5,000 (Approximately US$33)
J$10 million - J$19 million	J$10,000 (Approximately US$67)
J$20 million - J$29 million	J$15,000 (Approximately US$100)
J$30 million to J$39 million	J$20,000 (Approximately US$133)
J$40 million and above	J$25,000 (Approximately US$166)

$ Values calculated at approximate 2021 rates: *Conversion rate US$1 = Jamaican $150*

Stamp duty must be paid before one can obtain a grant to call in the assets of the estate, including life insurance policies and money in the bank. The Stamp Office will not refund any payment made at the previous rate of 3% of the value of the estate.

ATTORNEY'S FEES

Estates valued at a gross market value of less than J$250,000 (approximately US$1,666 in 2021) will incur attorney's fees at 5% of the value plus general consumption tax (GCT) of 16.5% (reduced to 15% announced in March 2020). For those over J$250,000, the rate is 3% plus GCT. Additionally, there is a 2% fee on the gross market value of the property plus GCT for properties transferred to beneficiaries. For preparing the affidavit to obtain the Commissioner General's assessment of transfer tax, there is a cost of J$80,000 (approximately US$533) plus GCT for Attorney's Fee.

The Fair Competition Act prevents attorney's fees from being subjected to the Bar Association's scale of fees. Attorneys set their rates inclusive of charges for advertising to invite creditors to the settlement of the estate, plus administrative expenses.

EXECUTOR'S FEES

The fee is six percent (6%) of all payments made by the executor regarding the estate. Some of these include debts, liabilities, management charges, expenses regarding dividends, interest, rent, receipts of any estate or trust, and on properties handled by him. Often in Jamaica, executors are family members or friends of the testator and may choose not to accept a fee for administering the will. If the executor is also a beneficiary, there is a chance he forfeits his fee. The six percent (6%) fee is divided equally on estates with more than one executor.

Executor's fees are not payable on properties owned by joint ownership as they do not fall under the terms of the will. They are therefore not administered by the executor.

TRANSFER TAXES ON PROPERTY

The Transfer Tax Act stipulates that properties willed to beneficiaries shall be considered equal to the market value of the properties at the date of death. Therefore, the transfer of property incurs transfer taxes of 1.5 percent of the real estate's market value at the date of death, minus funeral expenses, estate administration taxes, and debts related to the property, to a maximum of five percent (5%) of the value of the property. These costs will not be allowed if the estate can cover them from, for example, cash or life insurance. The final figure is taxed at 4% (a reduction from 7.5%). If it remains unpaid, interest on transfer taxes accrues at 6% per annum from twelve months after the death to the date that the taxes are paid. The Act further stipulates that all properties, including those owned overseas, are subject to tax in Jamaica. Transfer taxes must be paid before transferring any property to the beneficiaries.

The original threshold of J$100,000.00 (approximately US$666) meant that tax was due on property values above this figure. This low threshold and any due and accrued interest resulted in a prohibitive tax burden on property owners. The hardship resulted in several families being unable to pay the taxes, electing to live on the property and pass it from generation to generation. The threshold has been raised to J$10 million (US$66,666), so taxes become due on property values exceeding J$10 million. Beneficiaries should now be encouraged by this massive reduction in death duties to pursue the probate and transfer of their properties.

ETCHED IN MY MEMORY

Pay your taxes

Peter thought he was smart and even boasted how he had not been paying his taxes for many years. He bought his assets and lived a lavish lifestyle. One day, Peter was driving along the countryside; his car got out of control and faced him with an oncoming truck. It was a horrible accident, and he did not survive. He had a will in place, but it was not probated for years. His family was appalled at the deductions to cover overdue taxes plus interest for the many years the taxes remained unpaid.

Death and taxes are inevitable. Peter experienced both in short order. Always remember that interest is calculated on unpaid taxes, increasing one's liabilities which must be paid before the distribution of assets to beneficiaries.

5 INTESTACY & PROBATE

"It is up to us to live up to the legacy that was left for us, and to leave a legacy that is worthy of our children and of future generations."

Christine Gregoire

Probate refers to the process of settling a decedent's estate. Whether someone dies with or without a will, the estate requires the opening, administration, and closing of the estate, necessitating the payment of all taxes and other debts first and distributing the residuary estate to the beneficiaries. The main differences between intestate and testate estates lie in the responsibility for administering the estate and in determining the beneficiaries.

An estate with a valid will has a named executor charged with administering the estate and distributing assets to the named beneficiaries. The law of intestacy predetermines the beneficiaries in order of priority, and the court appoints an administrator to wind up an intestate estate.

Probate is necessary because there will be no legal way to transfer assets to beneficiaries without it. It also provides the opportunity to wind up a decedent's financial affairs.

How is a will probated? When there is a valid will, the court oversees the probate and determines if the will is legitimate. The executor is responsible for the probate of the will. He presents the will to the court and receives authorization to administer the estate. This process allows the executor to take control of the decedent's assets, pay any outstanding debts and taxes, file any tax or probate documents to the relevant government bodies, distribute the residuary estate to the beneficiaries, and close the estate.

The contesting of a will is reduced when the law is followed.

INTESTACY IN FLORIDA

The Florida Intestate Succession laws administer intestate estates. To have the estate administered, an "interested" person may file for Letters of Administration through the court, which appoints an administrator for the estate. Based on the evidence, the court approves the identities of the heirs.

The surviving spouse gets the first right to appointment as a personal representative. The inability or unwillingness of the surviving spouse to serve, or if the decedent was unmarried at the time of death, the heirs name a person or institution to get the second right. Without an agreement among them, the judge holds a hearing and decides.

The Basic Rules of Intestate Succession apply to intestacy estates. Under Florida law, an estate must undergo probate to pass assets from a decedent to their beneficiaries. Intestacy in Florida may be whole or in part. If a person did not leave a will or if his will is invalid, intestacy is considered whole. Partial intestacy occurs when a will exists but does not allow for distributing all the assets. Those with less than $75,000 in assets or estates where decedents have been dead for more than two years may use a faster probate process known as Summary Administration. Estates outside these criteria are probated under

Formal Administration, which is court-supervised and more time-consuming. Each estate that files for formal probate incurs a flat $400 fee.

Below is the predetermined priority order that Florida uses to distribute an intestate estate:

TABLE OF DISTRIBUTION For an intestate estate in Florida

Relationship	Inheritance
Children but no spouse	Children inherit everything
Spouse but no descendants	Spouse inherits everything
Spouse and descendants from you and that spouse, and the spouse has no other descendants	Spouse inherits everything
Spouse and descendants from you and that spouse, and the spouse has descendants from another relationship	Spouse inherits ½ of your intestate property. Your descendants inherit ½ of property, per stirpes*
Spouse, and descendants from you and someone other than that spouse	Spouse inherits ½ of your intestate property. Your descendants inherit ½ of your intestate property
Parents but no spouse or descendants	Parents inherit everything if alive; if not alive, property passes to siblings and their descendants, per stirpes
Siblings but no spouse, descendants or parents	Siblings inherit everything
None of the above alive	½ to heirs of decedent's maternal grandparents and their relatives, per stirpes ½ to heirs of decedent's paternal grandparents, per stirpes If no relatives on one side, the other side inherits everything

Source: Fla. Stat. Ann. § 732.101-104

* ***Per Stirpes***
A method of distributing the shares of an estate. It is assumed that each descendant is entitled to an equal share of an estate so, if one dies his share is divided equally among his descendants.

Half Relatives
Siblings with one shared parent are recognized as a whole and have the same right to intestate property as those with both parents in common.
Fla. Stat. Ann. § 732.105

Posthumous Relatives
Relatives conceived before and born after the decedent's death inherit as if they were born during his lifetime.
Fla. Stat. Ann. § 732.106

Immigration Status
A beneficiary on a will made in the United States is entitled to their inheritance, regardless of country of residence, or if they are legally in the US. For intestate estates, the rules regarding inheritance for undocumented persons differ by state. An attorney is best to advise on this topic
Stat. Ann. § 732.1101

Divorce
Divorce ends the right for a spouse to inherit. If, however, the marriage is not dissolved at the decedent's death, the surviving spouse will still inherit.

Disqualification
Murder of the decedent disqualifies the murderer from inheriting any share of the estate.
Fla. Stat. Ann. § 732.802

PROBATE IN FLORIDA

The following and other mention of Florida laws have not been approved by the Florida Bar or the State of Florida and should not be taken as legal advice. Remember always to seek the advice of an attorney and an estate planner on legal and estate planning matters.

PERSONAL REPRESENTATIVE

The executor of the estate in Florida is referred to as Personal Representative. They may be an individual/s or a corporation. The individual must be a Florida resident of direct lineage or close relative of the decedent. They cannot be convicted felons or be under the age of 18 and must be deemed mentally capable of performing the task of administering the estate.

Corporate entities allowed as personal representatives of an estate are banks, savings and loan institutions, or a trust company incorporated in Florida. Absent a will, the Florida Court will appoint a Personal Representative. Usually, it will first nominate the surviving spouse. If they do not agree to serve, the court will appoint the person designated by the beneficiaries. In case of a disagreement, the judge, after a hearing, will appoint a personal representative.

The personal representative should appoint an attorney, who will represent him and not the beneficiaries, to guide him through the probate process. He should also employ professionals in the respective areas to ensure he gets a professional and legal job done.

Duties of the Personal Representative

The duties of the Personal Representative include:

- Obtain several copies of the death certificate
- Apply for ten to twenty letters of qualification as executor
- Apply to IRS for Taxpayer Identification Number (EIN) for the estate (This replaces the decedent's social security number)
- Inform relevant persons and businesses of the death - Employer, Social Security, banks, credit card companies, credit bureaus, insurance companies, and pension companies, among others
- Identify the decedent's probate assets and have them valued
- Use the EIN to open a checking account in the name "Estate of......" and have the executor's name printed on checks. (Pay all bills by check)
- Locate all of the decedent's documents - Birth certificate, marriage certificate, bank accounts, insurance policies, credit cards, investment accounts, pension statements, last tax returns, online data to which the personal representative will have access
- Cancel subscriptions, memberships, and similar arrangements. Transfer utilities, car insurance, home insurance, and similar accounts to the surviving spouse or the estate
- Employ professionals to help administer the probate estate - attorney, accountant, appraiser, and investment adviser. The personal representative employs an attorney to cover their actions and not the estate
- Publish a notice addressed to creditors in the local newspaper, allowing them to make their claims within the required time
- Apply for due benefits, for example, life insurance proceeds, unpaid salary and other benefits from the employer, Social Security death and survivor benefits
- Serve a "Notice of Administration" providing information about the process, the procedure regarding how objections are to be handled

- Search for creditors and notify them of the timeline to submit claims
- Object to improper claims, and defend any filed suits
- Pay valid claims and expenses for administering the probate estate
- File tax returns and pay taxes
- Distribute to beneficiaries
- Close the probate estate

The process takes between a few weeks to a year or longer.

Duties of the Trustee

A trustee has the legal obligation to administer the trustor's wishes for their beneficiaries, acts as the legal owner of the trust assets and is responsible for handling those assets until transfer to the respective heirs.

Some of the duties of the trustee under Florida law include:

1) The duty to administer the trust in good faith, in accordance with the terms and purposes of the trust, and in the interests of the beneficiaries pursuant to *Fla. Stat. § 736.0801*
2) A duty of loyalty to the trust beneficiaries and administering the trust "solely in the interests of the beneficiaries" pursuant to *Fla. Stat. § 736.0802*
3) Administering the trust as a prudent person would, by considering the purposes, terms, distribution requirements, and other circumstances of the Trust, and shall exercise reasonable care, skill and caution *(Fla. Stat. § 736.0804)*
4) Taking steps to protect the trust property and assets (*Fla. Stat. §736.0809)*
5) A trustee who has special skills or expertise, or is named trustee in reliance on the trustee's representation that the trustee has special skills or expertise, shall use those special skills or expertise *(Stat. § 736.0806)*
6) Keeping proper, clear, distinct, and accurate records of the administration of the trust and keeping trust property separate from the trustee's property *(Stat. §736.0810)*
7) Keeping the qualified beneficiaries of the trust reasonably informed of the trust and its administration, and providing a qualified beneficiary with a complete copy of the trust instrument; providing a trust accounting, from the date of the last accounting or, if none, from the date on which the trustee became accountable, to each qualified beneficiary at least annually and on termination of the trust or change of the trustee *(Stat. §736.0813)*
8) Informing the beneficiaries of the trust about all monies, funds, assets, and personal property that came into his possession as trustee, and which were distributed, as well as to account for all assets, income, expenses, gains or losses of the trust pursuant to *Fla. Stat. §§ 736.08135*
9) Enforcing claims, defending actions to preserve trust property, and exercising reasonable care and skill in the administration of the trust pursuant to *Fla. Stat. §§ 736.0811 and 736.0816*

The notice of trust gives information about the decedent's identity as the grantor or settlor of the trust and names the current trustee. It also informs the decedent's creditors of the existence of the trust and their rights to claim against the assets of the trust. Filed notices allow the creditors to make their claims within sixty (60) days. When there is no filing, the creditors are allowed two years from the trustor's death to make their claims.

The trustor may also appoint the personal representative as the trustee. The trustee's duties are similar to those of the personal representative, except that they have fewer documents to file to the Clerk of the Court.

THE APPLICATION

The application for Formal Administration must include this documentation:

- The petitioner's name, address, interest in the estate, name, and address of the probate attorney
- The decedent's name, last known address, state and county of domicile, age at the time of death, last four digits of social security, and place of death
- The beneficiaries' names, addresses, dates of birth of any minors, and the relationship to the decedent
- The reason for filing and probating the decedent's estate in the chosen county
- The reason for choosing the personal representative and his qualifications to serve under Florida law
- A list of assets and their values and a declaration of whether the estate will be required to file a Federal Estate Tax return, IRS Form 706
- A declaration of whether the decedent had a will, any statement identifying unrevoked wills, and any codicils
- A declaration if the decedent did not have a will
- A declaration by the petitioner that he could not locate any will or codicil after a reasonable search
- A Waiver of Priority, Consent to Appointment, and Waiver of Notice and Bond signed by all beneficiaries indicating that they are not contesting or planning to contest the decedent's will
- Original Death Certificate
- Original Last Will and Testament. No copies accepted

TYPES OF PROBATE

There are four different types of probates in Florida, each selected based on the circumstances of the decedent's estate.

DISPOSITION WITHOUT ADMINISTRATION

This form is not regarded as a form of probate. In the event the decedent dies leaving very little, it reimburses, from the estate, the person who pays for the funeral and medical expenses for the last sixty days before the death.

To request reimbursement, a "Disposition of Personal Property Without Administration" is filed, complete with a certified copy of the death certificate, bills, receipts, and the filing fee.

ANCILLARY ADMINISTRATION

Ancillary Administration is used when the decedent owned property, for example, vacation homes, in Florida but was not a Florida resident. An experienced attorney is best suited for this transaction, which involves transferring the Florida property at the same time when the primary probate proceedings are happening in a different state.

SUMMARY ADMINISTRATION

Estates with less than $75,000 in assets or estates where decedents have been dead for over two years may use a faster probate process known as Summary Administration. Estates outside these criteria are probated under Formal Administration, which is court-supervised and more time-consuming.

The form must state the assets, their values, and the beneficiaries and must be signed and verified by the surviving spouse. If a beneficiary does not sign, the court must notify him of the filing. On approval, the court issues a release of the assets to the beneficiaries.

With summary administration, the court does not appoint a personal representative. Once the estate qualifies for summary probate, the court issues an order to distribute the assets directly to the lawful beneficiaries.

FORMAL ADMINISTRATION

Formal Administration is the most common type of probate proceeding in Florida. The court accepts the person named in the will, once they meet all the criteria set by the law to do the job. If the court considers the will legally valid, the personal representative follows the decedent's wishes as outlined in the will. Once appointed, the court regards the estate as "opened" and issues Letters of Administration.

The personal representative needs to:

- File the original will with the Clerk of the Florida Circuit Court in the county where the testator lived within ten days of death
- Provide two death certificates, bank statements, tax returns, titles for properties, retirement account statements, life insurance policies, and any mortgage notes or other documents that may be requested of him by the court
- Personal Representative then requests the court to probate the will by filing a Petition of Administration and receiving Letters of Administration, allowing the payment of all taxes and other debts on behalf of the deceased, distribution of the remaining assets to the beneficiaries.
- Report to the court.

Florida courts recognize a self-proving will that conforms to the law. It confirms that the testator and witnesses signed an affidavit in the presence of a notary public confirming the validity of their signatures on the will. If they did not sign an affidavit at the time of signing and witnessing the will, one witness could sign under oath, guaranteeing the authenticity of the signatures.

The personal representative then files a report to the court detailing actions accounting for all income and expenditure and providing receipts for these transactions.

The Clerk of the Court gives a copy to all interested parties who have thirty days to object to any aspect of the accounting. The court then holds a hearing to approve the accounting formally. The personal representative then files a petition for discharge of the estate and, on completion of all transactions, is relieved of further responsibilities. The estate is then closed by the court.

THE PROCESS

A circuit court judge presides over probate proceedings. If the decedent had a will, the court would decide whether the nominated personal representative is qualified to serve in the position and rule on the will's validity. If the person or institution meets the statutory qualifications, the judge will issue "Letters of Administration," authorizing them to administer the decedent's estate. If there are questions or disputes during the probate, the judge will hold a hearing to resolve the matter, and the decision will be in a written direction called an "order."

The documents needed to begin the probate process must be filed with the Clerk of the Court in the county of the decedent's residence within ten days of death, and the personal representative at the time of filing, must pay the filing fee. In years past, all the information submitted for the Florida probate process was available for public scrutiny; however, in recent years, private financial information regarding the estate is no longer open to the public.

Probate also winds up the decedent's financial affairs. A submitted will to the court and probate are necessary to pass ownership of probate assets to the decedent's beneficiaries. Many estates in Florida avoid probate for several reasons. The values may be less than the allowed threshold; property owners organize their portfolios using trusts, life insurance, and retirement packages with named beneficiaries; or own property by joint tenancy.

Although there is no fee for depositing the will with the Clerk of Court, the personal representative must pay a filing fee once the case opens. Each estate that files for formal probate incurs a flat $400 fee. The process takes between three months and years, depending on the complexity of the estate.

ATTORNEY'S FEES

Florida sets out the attorney's fees that it presumes reasonable based on the value of the assets which go through probate, plus any income earned during the probate proceeding.

The statutory attorney's fees are as follows:

Value of Estate US$	Approximately US$
Up to $40,000	$1,500
$40,000 to $70,000	$2,250
$70,000 to $100,000	$3,000
$100,000 to $1Million	$3,000, plus 3% of the value over $100,000
$1 million to $3 million	$30,000, plus 2.5% of the value over $1 million
$3 million to $5 million	$50,000, plus 2% of the value above $3 million
$5 million to $10 million	$90,000, plus 1.5% on the value above $5 million
More than $10 million	$165,000, plus 1% of the value above $10 million

Source: Fla. Stat. Ann. § 733.6171.

The fees may be higher for additional work. Some attorneys, however, do not abide by these rates but set a flat fee, for example:

Summary Administration	Probate fees start at US$1,000
Formal Administration	Probate fees start from US$1,500 plus other costs related to income earned during probate proceedings
Filing the case Petition for Summary Administration	US$345
Filing fees for Formal Administration	US$400 + cost associated with bonds for personal, copy and certification representatives of court records + advertising costs + publication costs

Administering one's estate can be expensive. Adequately preparing for its payment is advised.

PERSONAL REPRESENTATIVE'S COMPENSATION

There are several ways to calculate the personal representative's compensation. It can be stated in the will, in a contract between the decedent and the personal representative, an agreement between the personal representative and those responsible for payment, or determined by a judge.

Under Florida law, the figure must be a reasonable fee commensurate with the job.

INTESTACY IN JAMAICA

In an intestate estate in Jamaica, the proper applicants to the estate are the decedent's beneficiaries over age eighteen. The spouse and children are the primary beneficiaries.

The Administrator-General is assigned the responsibility to be the executor of an intestate estate, and, if there are minor children, assumes the role of trustee.

The Administrator-General's certificate must accompany all applications for a grant of Letters of Administration. Once the court issues the Grant of Administration, the Administrator-General administers the estate. Her duties are similar to those of an executor:

- Collecting assets
- Paying debts
- Requesting the release of titles to properties owned by the decedent from all institutions that hold those titles.
- Placing an advertisement in the newspaper inviting creditors of the estate to substantiate their claim within six weeks after the publication of the advertisement
- Paying all statutory debts. Transfer taxes are due on real property, shares, and stocks after allowance for funeral expenses and mortgage debts. They must pay these before the sale of the related asset
- Paying legitimate claims. They must pay these before distribution to beneficiaries. If there are insufficient cash assets to settle the claims, the Administrator-General may exercise her power to sell the property to meet these debts. There would be no transfer tax if a property were the principal place of residence for the decedent and the applicant at the time of death or on the matrimonial home where the spouse is the applicant
- Managing, investing, and preserving all assets until all minors attain the age of majority
- If the decedent was a majority shareholder in a company, registering as a shareholder in respect of his shares and performing all duties to preserve the values of the shares for the beneficiaries, for example, attending general meetings.
- Assisting with educational, medical, and other crucial expenses of minor beneficiaries using 50% of their capital entitlement during their minority years; and
- Distributing the assets to beneficiaries

The administrator may commission 6% of the estate's value before attorney's fees and the distribution to the beneficiaries.

When the last minor attains the age of eighteen and all debts are settled, they will produce a final Statement of Account with the income and expenditure, the entitlement to each beneficiary, and a Method of Payment Form outlining the payment options available to the beneficiaries. The disbursements follow once the beneficiaries sign and approve the Statement of Account and the payment method. Beneficiaries living overseas, for example, may elect to receive bank drafts, and those living in Jamaica may elect payment by check sent by registered mail.

Amendments to the Administrator-General's Act, since 1999, do not mandate the Administrator-General to act in cases where the beneficiaries are all adults. Those in disagreement have a right to apply to the court for an order. The Administrator-General advises them that if they wish, they can apply for one of them to apply for the Letters of Administration. Once she is satisfied, the named person applies, and she issues a certificate agreeing to the granting of Letters of Administration.

TABLE OF DISTRIBUTION Jamaica

The Intestate's Estate and Property Charges Act of 1937, amended in 2015, lays out the order of priority of an intestate estate along with the respective entitlement of the applicants. Excerpts from the Act show the relationship to the decedent and the proportions of the residuary estate they would inherit.

If the decedent has no one in a category on the predetermined list of beneficiaries, the asset is passed to the next of kin in the next following category. Below is an example of distributing an intestate estate in Jamaica:

Relationship	Inheritance
Spouse, children and parents	½ to spouse ½ to children in equal shares If only 1 child, 2/3 to the spouse, 1/3 to the child. (Parents do not share in the estate)
Children and parents only	Children take absolutely in equal shares (Parents do not share in the estate)
Spouse and parents only	2/3 to spouse 1/3 to parents (in equal share if both alive)
Parents survive, but no spouse	Parents take absolutely in equal shares, or children of single surviving parent take absolutely

The class of persons next in line in the previous table will take in equal share in the following order to the exclusion of those in the lower classes:
If no spouse, children or parent

1 Brothers and sisters of the whole blood

2 Brothers and sisters of the half-blood

3. Grandparents

4. Uncles and aunts of the whole blood

5. Uncles and aunts of the half-blood

6. The Crown (as Bona Vacantia)

Bona Vacantia, which is the Latin for "ownerless goods," refers to property that has no owner.

Spouse:

For succession, a spouse includes an unmarried person who cohabited with the deceased for not less than five (5) years immediately before his/her death. The spouse will also need to obtain a Declaration from the Court stating that they are the spouse of the deceased. Additionally, the spouse is also entitled to all personal chattels absolutely (provided they were not being used by the deceased in the course of business). Personal chattels include, inter alia, motor vehicles, jewelry, painting, and furniture. The spouse is further entitled to $10,000.00 or 1/10 of the net estate (whichever is greater), as an absolute interest, with interest thereon at a rate of 10% until paid.

(Source: https://agd.gov.jm)

THE PROCESS

The administrator of an intestate estate must obtain:

- Confirmation of the assets of the decedent for the Administrator-General
- Confirmation from decedent's former employers of the employee's benefits, unpaid salary, vacation leave pay, gratuity, National Insurance, and National Housing Trust contributions
- Confirmation from financial institutions and individuals regarding funds, stocks, shares, debentures, and investments for the decedent
- Details of life insurance policy contract/s
- Statement of Account from the bank and other financial institutions
- Share certificates
- Information on property ownership, outstanding mortgage, and mortgage insurance
- Original Duplicate Certificate of Title for land
- Purchase receipts and agreement for sales (where title was not issued to the decedent)
- Conveyance
- Deed of Gift
- Indenture
- Motor vehicle Certificate of Title, Fitness, and Registration. If the vehicle was not predominantly used for commercial purposes, it is transferable to the spouse as personal chattel.

APPLICATION FOR THE GRANT OF LETTERS OF ADMINISTRATION

The executor applies for a Grant of Administration from the Resident Magistrate's Court or the Supreme Court to allow the Administrator-General to access, collect, transfer, sell, or otherwise the decedent's assets. They apply for the Letters of Administration for estates valued at up to J$1,500,000 to the Resident Magistrate's Court and to the Supreme Court for estates valued over J$3,000,000.

The application must be accompanied by:

- Copy of the Death Certificate or an Affidavit completed by a person who was acquainted with the decedent and attended the funeral
- Funds to stamp the documents. (To stamp the Oath of Administration costs J$5,000)
- Funds to stamp the Grant of Letters of Administration (J$5,000 to J$25,000 dependent on the value of the estate)

Under the 1999 amendment to the Administrator-General's Act, The Administrator-General has the power to request the release of funds from institutions holding funds for the estate, which will assist the beneficiaries in meeting the application costs.

PROBATE IN JAMAICA

The attorney acting for the intended applicant/administrator will need to submit these documents to the Administrator-General's Department to support an application for the certificate:

- Particulars required for the Administrator-General, completed and signed before a Justice of the Peace
- Proof of death (certified copy of death certificate preferred)
- Oath of the administrator(s) for Letters of Administration prepared by the retained attorney
- Consent of person entitled in priority, if the applicant does not have the prior right to apply
- Order declaring the applicant the lawful spouse of the deceased, for persons involved in common-law union (must first meet specific requirements)

- The applicable fee. When the Administrator-General receives the requisite documents and information, she will issue a certificate. The attorney-at-law will submit this and other documents to the relevant court for a grant of Letters of Administration.
- Once the grant is issued, the appointed administrator(s) will follow the normal process of administration.

NO PROBATE NECESSARY

Not all assets need probate. Depending on the structure of an estate, it may bypass the probate process. Assets in this category include properties and other jointly owned assets, which would transfer to the surviving owner. Examples of this would consist of properties owned by joint tenancy, joint bank accounts, assets in a trust, and assets with named beneficiaries, for example, life insurance, and retirement accounts.

DYING TESTATE

The executor's job begins after the testator's death starting with getting the court to examine and confirm that the will meets the requirements of the Wills Act. The executor then collects originals of all documents needed to administer the estate, including death certificates, the will, life insurance policies, certificates of title, share certificates, bank records, and receipts of funeral expenses, among others. The services of an attorney is then sought to apply to the court for a Grant of Probate of the will, during which period the property cannot be sold or transferred. The executor provides the required documentation and signs the will in the presence of a Justice of the Peace, pays the stamp duty at the Stamp Office, applies for the Grant of Probate, and pays the estate duties to effect property transfer to the beneficiaries.

After the grant of probate, they must place advertisements in the amount of approximately J$15,000 in the newspaper with notices requesting creditors to make legitimate claims on the estate. The tax is paid within one year after death to avoid accumulating interest at 6% of the estate's value per annum, from the end of the first year to the payment date. If the will or the circumstances under which the testator died is undergoing legal action, they may meet additional costs that must be paid before distributing assets.

The executor pays all other liabilities, then files a record of the accounts for the estate with the court. The court registrar sends copies of the reports to the heirs and creditors for acknowledgment, and if there are no disputes, the estate is closed.

6

READY TO PREPARE YOUR SIMPLE WILL?

SPECIAL POINTS TO REMEMBER WHEN WRITING YOUR WILL

"We don't inherit the earth from our ancestors, we borrow it from our children."

David Brower

Ready to write a simple will? Do this simple test:

- Testator is at least 18 years of age - Check Yes.
- Testator is of sound mind - Check Yes.
- Testator is being forced to write the will - Check No
- Testator confirms action is free of fraud - Check Yes.

Having passed the test, the testator ensures the validity of the will and is now ready to begin the process.

1. List all assets
2. List all liabilities
3. List all beneficiaries
4. List the assignment of the assets to the selected beneficiaries
5. Remember to check the relevant laws in the respective area for topics like the types of wills accepted, stipulations, and probate

Below are some reminders to help in preparing your simple will:

Executor - *Reminders*

- Select the executor/s and get their agreement to accept the job and all its responsibilities (Name a second executor in case the first might not be able to serve at the time of death)
- The executor is due a percentage of the estate as payment but may choose not to accept payment (Allow for the fee)
- Give a copy of the will to the executor/s and discuss any special instructions with them
- An executor may be a beneficiary but not a witness to the will

Guardian for minor children - *Reminders*

- Select a qualified guardian for minor children, if any
- Get agreement to accept the responsibilities
- A guardian may also be a trustee, but separating the responsibilities is recommended
  - Name of guardian should be in both spouse's wills

Trustee for minor children - ***Reminders***

- Select the trustee for minor children, if any (Select an individual or a trust company to take care of the financial aspects of children's lives)
- The guardian may also be the trustee (Separate the roles, if possible)
  - If leaving a minor as a beneficiary, name the trustee giving the responsibility of managing funds
  - Name of trustee should be in both spouse's wills

Liabilities - ***Reminders***

- Liabilities are paid first
- Never forget tax liabilities
  - Liabilities +Assignment to beneficiaries = Assets needed

Assets - ***Reminders***

- List all assets; remember digital assets and foreign assets (The rules of intestacy will govern unaccounted assets)
- Do not forget assets that are already assigned
- Receivables are assets. Decide on debts to be forgiven, if any
- Decide if any assets should be sold to add cash to the estate
- Life insurance adds value to a portfolio. Have a professional life agent or estate planner assess the portfolio and determine life insurance needs

Features of a will - ***Reminders***

- A will form or template is not necessary to write a will (options are available to make the process easier)
- A will is ambulatory - can be changed at any time during one's lifetime
- A codicil amends parts of a will

Contents of a will - ***Reminders***

- Pay special attention to items that one should include in a will
- Delete items not to be included in a will
- Pay special attention to types of property ownership (ensure one has the legal right to transfer assets)
  - Property owned by joint tenancy may be included in a will with a statement declaring the type of ownership and a potential beneficiary
  - Include assets from an unprobated will
  - Assign property - Listing all beneficiaries will overlook none of the intended beneficiaries
- Disinheriting heirs - List disinherited heirs to prevent a challenge as an oversight
- Use percentages for the allocation of assets
  - They account for changes in the asset values
  - They help to show one's intent in case of a shortfall in assets
  - They assist the court with significant decisions
- Residuary Clause - Do not forget the residuary clause with a named beneficiary or beneficiaries to capture any unmentioned assets

Sign and date the will - *Reminders*

- A will must be signed and dated by the testator and two witnesses in the presence of each other
- A witness does not have to know the contents of a will. Their job is to witness the testator's signature
- An executor can be a beneficiary
- A witness cannot be a beneficiary
- If the will form includes a self-proving affidavit, it must be notarized

General

- The estate planner or attorney needs to be consulted for complex estates
- Talk to the estate planner about ways to structure the estate to save on taxes

GET INFORMATION TOGETHER

- From the information gleaned, one can now decide whether their estate will require a simple will that protects its validity and incontestability or the services of an attorney or estate planner to prepare their more complex will
- For a simple will, look back at *Chapter 3* and the reminders above, then put data in the form overleaf:

COLLECTING THE DATA FOR A SIMPLE WILL

Do I already have a will? Yes ☐ No ☐

Do I need to update my will? Yes ☐ No ☐

Executors

Choices for my Executors	Contact
____________________	____________________
____________________	____________________
Date to meet with Executors	____________________

Guardian

Choices for the Guardian of my minor children	Contact
____________________	____________________
____________________	____________________
Date to meet with Guardian	____________________

Trustee

Choices for Trustee	Contact
____________________	____________________
____________________	____________________
Date to meet with Trustee	____________________

Witnesses

	Contact
____________________	____________________
____________________	____________________

Beneficiaries	Relationship

List of my Assets	Value
Total Value	

List of my Liabilities	Amount
Total Liabilities	
Net Worth (*Assets - Liabilities*)	

Defining my legacy

Asset	Address/Location	Beneficiary
___	___	___
___	___	___
___	___	___
___	___	___
___	___	___
___	___	___
___	___	___

Special Requests

Do I want to be an organ donor? Yes ☐ No ☐ Details ___

___

___

Funeral Preferences

Funeral Home Name ___

Address ___

Telephone/Email ___

Type of Funeral Public ☐ Private ☐

Cremation/Inurnment Yes ☐ No ☐

Earth Burial Yes ☐ No ☐

Other Yes ☐ No ☐

Church ___

Officiating Minister ___

Address ___

Phone Number/Email ___

Special Requests (cont'd)

Cemetery ____________________

Address ____________________

Phone Number/Email ____________________

Hymns ____________________

____

____

Musician ____________________

Soloist ____________________

Ceremony	Yes ☐	No ☐
Donations to be made to (*Organization*)	Yes ☐	No ☐
Flowers	Yes ☐	No ☐
Special request for colors	Yes ☐	No ☐
Repast	Yes ☐	No ☐

Other Requests (Military involvement)

I am a Military Veteran

Service Number	Branch	Rank
____________________	____________________	____________________

Date Enlisted	Date Discharged
____________________	____________________

Persons To Be Notified Of My Death

Name ____________________

Address ____________________

____

Relationship ____________________

Telephone/Email ____________________

Name ____________________

Address ____________________

____

Relationship ____________________

Telephone/Email ____________________

Name ____________________

Address ____________________

____

Relationship ____________________

Telephone/Email ____________________

Name ____________________

Address ____________________

____

Relationship ____________________

Telephone/Email ____________________

Persons To Be Notified Of My Death (cont'd)

Name ______________________________

Address ______________________________

____

Relationship ______________________________

Telephone/Email ______________________________

Name ______________________________

Address ______________________________

____

Relationship ______________________________

Telephone/Email ______________________________

Name ______________________________

Address ______________________________

____

Relationship ______________________________

Telephone/Email ______________________________

Name ______________________________

Address ______________________________

____

Relationship ______________________________

Telephone/Email ______________________________

WILL TEMPLATES

Although a form is not required to write a will, it should contain all the valid will requirements. There are, however, several templates that can be used to assist with writing a will.

- Preprinted forms - These forms require completing the blank spaces. Two samples of preprinted simple wills are in Appendices 1 and 2.

  Appendix 1 is a simple will template widely used in Jamaica and may be purchased at pharmacies, bookshops, or post offices.

  Appendix 2 represents a Florida Last Will and Testament for use in the preparation of a simple will in Florida.
- Statutory forms - Some states have a simple will form written into their state law to provide a simple and cost-effective way for its citizens to prepare a will accepted in a probate court. These are available in California, Maine, Michigan, New Mexico, and Wisconsin.
- Will software - The program prepares the will when the testator downloads an estate planning software on a computer and inputs the requested information
- Online will programs - The testator visits a website, answers the questions asked, and the computer creates the will online. This process is similar to the will software, except the testator does not download the software

Testators who feel comfortable having their will prepared for them online may wish to visit:

Electronic Forms LLC at www.eforms.com
Free fillable forms are also available!

Whatever works best, use it and get the will done today!

ETCHED IN MY MEMORY

Use Percentages to gift property

Many years ago, when property costs were way below current values, Mr. Josephs, in his will, wrote, "On the sale of my home I leave to my son, John, the sum of J$250,000 and the balance I leave for my son Christopher."

Based on the relationship between him and his sons and the values of properties then, it was clear that his intention was for the more significant portion to pass to John. Mr. Josephs lived for many years after he wrote his will, and, over the years, he never had it updated.

Little did he know that the value of real estate would have escalated exponentially. On the probate of his will, John received J$250,000 and Christopher got the remaining millions of dollars.

Mr. Josephs' mistake is a vivid reminder always to use percentages when allocating assets in a will. It ensures that all beneficiaries receive their intended portion of an estate, even if the values change.

It also shows the testator's intent and serves as a guide for distributing the assets in the event there is a shortfall.

7 PREPPING FOR YOUR ESTATE PLANNING MEETING

"But if any provide not for his own, and specially for those of his own house, he hath denied the faith, and is worse than an infidel."

Timothy 5:8

Having a sizable and more complex estate involving businesses, multiple families, the need for advanced tax planning, and other issues requires the services of an attorney or an estate planner familiar with the laws relating to wills in a specific area. Employing their services will ensure that the will is done professionally to prevent complications after death.

The testator needs to prepare before meeting with the attorney or estate planner. The following pages provide a guide to assist with the preparation. Completing it will prepare the testator for the meeting with their attorney or estate planner. Let us do this!

PREPARATION NOTES FOR THE ESTATE OF

______________________________ Date__________

Persons To Be Notified Of My Death

Name ______________________________

Address ______________________________

____

Relationship ______________________________

Telephone/Email ______________________________

Name ______________________________

Address ______________________________

____

Relationship ______________________________

Telephone/Email ______________________________

Name ______________________________

Address ______________________________

____

Relationship ______________________________

Telephone/Email ______________________________

Name ______________________________

Address ______________________________

____

Relationship ______________________________

Telephone/Email ______________________________

Persons To Be Notified Of My Death (cont'd)

Name ______________________________

Address ______________________________

____

Relationship ______________________________

Telephone/Email ______________________________

Name ______________________________

Address ______________________________

____

Relationship ______________________________

Telephone/Email ______________________________

Name ______________________________

Address ______________________________

____

Relationship ______________________________

Telephone/Email ______________________________

Name ______________________________

Address ______________________________

____

Relationship ______________________________

Telephone/Email ______________________________

Persons/Companies to be contacted

Executor/s ______________________________

Address ______________________________

____

Telephone/Email ______________________________

Accountant ______________________________

Address ______________________________

____

Telephone/Email ______________________________

Attorney 1 ______________________________

Address ______________________________

____

Telephone/Email ______________________________

Attorney 2 ______________________________

Address ______________________________

____

Telephone/Email ______________________________

Investment Officer 1 ______________________________

Address ______________________________

____

Telephone/Email ______________________________

Persons/Companies to be contacted (cont'd)

Investment Officer 2 ______________________________

Address ______________________________

____

Telephone/Email ______________________________

Bank (*Personal*) ______________________________

Address ______________________________

____

Name on Account ______________________________

Type of Account ______________________________

Bank Account # ______________________________

Bank Card # ______________________________

Pin # ______________________________

Online Password ______________________________

Credit Card # ______________________________

Expiration Date ______________________________

Code ______________________________

Bank (*Personal*) ______________________________

Address ______________________________

____

Name on Account ______________________________

Type of Account ______________________________

Bank Account # ______________________________

Persons/Companies to be contacted (cont'd)

Bank Card # ______________________

Pin # ______________________

Online Password ______________________

Credit Card # ______________________

Expiration Date ______________________

Code ______________________

Checklist (Attach Copies)

Personal

Social Security (SS) # ______________________

Taxpayer Registration Number (TRN)# ______________________

SS/TRN Card Attached ______________________

Permanent Resident Card # ______________ Expiration Date______________

Passport # ______________ Expiration Date______________

Birth Certificate ______________________

Marriage Certificate/s ______________________

Divorce Papers ______________________

Driver's License # ______________ Expiration Date______________

Location of will ______________________

Investment Portfolio ______________________

____

____

____

Checklist (cont'd)

Life Insurance

Policy # ______________________________

Face Amount ______________________________

Beneficiary ______________________________

Policy # ______________________________

Face Amount ______________________________

Beneficiary ______________________________

Policy # ______________________________

Face Amount ______________________________

Beneficiary ______________________________

Policy # ______________________________

Face Amount ______________________________

Beneficiary ______________________________

Workplace Insurance
Policy # ______________________________

Face Amount ______________________________

Beneficiary ______________________________

Disability Insurance
Policy # ______________________________

Face Amount ______________________________

Beneficiary ______________________________

Long Term Care
Insurance Policy # ______________________________

Benefit ______________________________

Checklist (cont'd)

General Insurance Home *(Copies of contracts and Titles)*

Type of Coverage ____________________

Address of Property ____________________

Insurance Company ____________________

Type of Coverage ____________________

Address of Property ____________________

Insurance Company ____________________

Type of Coverage ____________________

Address of Property ____________________

Insurance Company ____________________

General Insurance Auto *(Copy of contract)*

Vehicle ____________________

Details ____________________

Insurance Company ____________________

Vehicle ____________________

Details ____________________

Insurance Company ____________________

Vehicle ____________________

Details ____________________

Insurance Company ____________________

Mortgage Information

Property ____________________

Lender ____________________

Checklist (cont'd)

Property ______________________

Lender ______________________

Property ______________________

Lender ______________________

Trust

Recipient ______________________

Trustee ______________________

Recipient ______________________

Trustee ______________________

Power of Attorney ______________________

Living Will ______________________

Letter of Wishes ______________________

Medical Records ______________________

Refills at Pharmacy ______________________

Contact List/Database ______________________

Checklist (cont'd)

Permission for executor to access online accounts *(letters to be done)*

Facebook ______________________

LinkedIn ______________________

Twitter ______________________

YouTube ______________________

Email ______________________

Affiliate Programs ______________________

Digital Accounts

Credit card cash back program ______________________

Frequent Flier Miles ______________________

Account ______________________

Online Digital Payments *(Automatic)*

____

____

____

Social Media Passwords

Facebook ______________________

LinkedIn ______________________

Twitter ______________________

Other ______________________

Other ______________________

Wishes For My Online Social Media Pages

Facebook ______________________

LinkedIn ______________________

Twitter ______________________

Other ______________________

Digital Accounts (cont'd)

Other Online Accounts with Passwords

Email 1 ______________________________

Email 2 ______________________________

Email 3 ______________________________

Cloud Storage ______________________________

Dropbox ______________________________

Other Digital Assets ______________________________

____

____

____

Business 1

Name of Business ______________________________

Address ______________________________

____

Social Security ______________________ Tax ID______________________

Location of company documents ______________________________

Online Sales Account/s_ ______________________________

Websites ______________________________

____

Bank *(Business)* ______________________________

Address ______________________________

____

Name on Account ______________________________

Type of Account ______________________________

Bank Account # ______________________________

Bank Card # ______________________________

Pin # ______________________________

Online Password ______________________________

Credit Card # ______________________________

Expiration Date ______________________________

Code ______________________________

Safety-Deposit Details ______________________________

Business 1 (cont'd)

Bank *(Business)* ______________________________

Address ______________________________

____

Name on Account ______________________________

Type of Account ______________________________

Bank Account # ______________________________

Bank Card # ______________________________

Pin # ______________________________

Online Password ______________________________

Credit Card # ______________________________

Expiration Date ______________________________

Code ______________________________

Safety-Deposit Details ______________________________

Investment Portfolio ______________________________

____

____

____

Life Insurance

Life Insurance Policy # ______________________________

Face Amount ______________________________

Beneficiary ______________________________

Business 1 (cont'd)

Life Insurance Policy # ______________________

Face Amount ______________________

Beneficiary ______________________

Life Insurance Policy # ______________________

Face Amount ______________________

Beneficiary ______________________

Life Insurance Policy # ______________________

Face Amount ______________________

Beneficiary ______________________

Workplace Insurance Policy # ______________________

Face Amount ______________________

Beneficiary ______________________

Disability Insurance Policy # ______________________

Face Amount ______________________

Beneficiary ______________________

Long Term Care Insurance Policy # ______________________

Benefit ______________________

General Insurance Property *(Copies of contracts and Titles)*

Type of Coverage ______________________

Address of Property ______________________

Insurance Company ______________________

Type of Coverage ______________________

Business 1 (cont'd)

Address of Property ______________________________

Insurance Company ______________________________

Type of Coverage ______________________________

Address of Property ______________________________

Insurance Company ______________________________

Mortgage Information

Property ______________________________

Lender ______________________________

Property ______________________________

Lender ______________________________

Property ______________________________

Lender ______________________________

General Insurance Auto *(Copy of contract)*

Vehicle ______________________________

Details ______________________________

Insurance Company ______________________________

Vehicle ______________________________

Details ______________________________

Insurance Company ______________________________

Vehicle ______________________________

Details ______________________________

Insurance Company ______________________________

Business 1 (cont'd)

Business Social Media Pages

Facebook ______________________ Password______________

LinkedIn ______________________ Password______________

Twitter ______________________ Password______________

YouTube ______________________ Password______________

Other ______________________ Password______________

Digital and Marketing Documents

Logo ______________________________________

Photos ______________________________________

Graphics ______________________________________

Audio Files ______________________________________

Video Presentations ______________________________________

Blogs ______________________________________

Marketing Materials ______________________________________

Other ______________________________________

Marketplace Accounts

Amazon ______________________________________

Etsy ______________________________________

Ebay ______________________________________

Go Daddy ______________________________________

Paypal ______________________________________

Western Union ______________________________________

Other ______________________________________

Business 1 (cont'd)

Online Subscriptions *(Automatic)*

Intellectual Property

Patent

Business 2

Name of Business ______________________

Address ______________________

____

Social Security ______________ Tax ID______________

Location of company documents ______________________

Online Sales Account/s_ ______________________

Websites ______________________

____

Bank *(Business)* ______________________

Address ______________________

____

Name on Account ______________________

Type of Account ______________________

Bank Account # ______________________

Bank Card # ______________________

Pin # ______________________

Online Password ______________________

Credit Card # ______________________

Expiration Date ______________________

Code ______________________

Safety-Deposit Details ______________________

Business 2 (cont'd)

Bank *(Business)* ______________________________

Address ______________________________

____

Name on Account ______________________________

Type of Account ______________________________

Bank Account # ______________________________

Bank Card # ______________________________

Pin # ______________________________

Online Password ______________________________

Credit Card # ______________________________

Expiration Date ______________________________

Code ______________________________

Safety-Deposit Details ______________________________

Investment Portfolio ______________________________

____

____

____

Life Insurance

Policy # ______________________________

Face Amount ______________________________

Beneficiary ______________________________

Business 2 (cont'd)

Policy # ______________________

Face Amount ______________________

Beneficiary ______________________

Policy # ______________________

Face Amount ______________________

Beneficiary ______________________

Policy # ______________________

Face Amount ______________________

Beneficiary ______________________

Workplace Insurance

Policy # ______________________

Face Amount ______________________

Beneficiary ______________________

Disability Insurance

Policy # ______________________

Coverage ______________________

Benefits ______________________

Long Term Care Insurance

Policy # ______________________

Benefits ______________________

General Insurance Property *(Copies of contracts and Titles)*

Type of Coverage ______________________

Address of Property ______________________

Insurance Company ______________________

Type of Coverage ______________________

Business 2 (cont'd)

Address of Property ______________________________

Insurance Company ______________________________

Type of Coverage ______________________________

Address of Property ______________________________

Insurance Company ______________________________

Mortgage Information

Property ______________________________

Lender ______________________________

Property ______________________________

Lender ______________________________

Property ______________________________

Lender ______________________________

General Insurance Auto *(Copy of contract)*

Vehicle ______________________________

Details ______________________________

Insurance Company ______________________________

Vehicle ______________________________

Details ______________________________

Insurance Company ______________________________

Vehicle ______________________________

Details ______________________________

Insurance Company ______________________________

Business 2 (cont'd)

Business Social Media Pages

Facebook ______________________ Password______________

LinkedIn ______________________ Password______________

Twitter ______________________ Password______________

YouTube ______________________ Password______________

Other ______________________ Password______________

Digital and Marketing Documents

Logo ______________________

Photos ______________________

Graphics ______________________

Audio Files ______________________

Video Presentations ______________________

Blogs ______________________

Marketing Materials ______________________

Other ______________________

Marketplace Accounts

Amazon ______________________

Etsy ______________________

Ebay ______________________

Go Daddy ______________________

Paypal ______________________

Western Union ______________________

Other ______________________

Business 2 (cont'd)

Online Subscriptions *(Automatic)* ____________________

____

____

Intellectual Property ____________________

____

____

Patent ____________________

____

____

8 FOR DISCUSSION WITH YOUR ESTATE PLANNER/ ATTORNEY

"Immortality is to live your life doing good things and leaving your mark behind."

Brandon Lee

Writing a will is but one aspect of estate planning, and although some rules relating to the writing of wills are universal, some may differ by territory, even between states in the US.

In addition to the prepared information, these are some reminders for discussion with the attorney or estate planner to ensure that the advisor covers all of the wishes.

Some suggestions for discussion:

- **Family situation**
  - Any special requirements for spouse and children, if any?
  - Children from a previous marriage or relationship?
  - Leaving an inheritance for an ex-spouse to care for children
  - Ages of children
  - Plans for the care of minor children
  - Using trusts as part of estate planning
  - Persons other than close family members to receive a legacy
- **Local real estate**
  - Residential property
  - Additional local properties
  - Treatment of properties
  - Properties owned by joint tenancy or tenancy in common?
- **Foreign property**
  - Property ownership in another state or country
  - Laws affecting property ownership in those states or country
  - Guidelines if a separate will is required
- **Financial**
  - Calculation of assets to cover liabilities and leave a legacy
  - Any legacy from unprobated will
  - Amount needed to cover any shortage
  - How to cover any shortfall
  - Any need to sell any assets
  - Calculation of net worth
- **Laws governing gift-giving**
  - To spouses
  - To other beneficiaries
  - Any threshold for family

- **Legal treatment of charitable giving**
  - Threshold
  - Effect on taxes
  - Annual gift-giving
- **Plans for your business**
  - Disclose partners, if any
  - Family members who work in the business
  - Current state of company records
  - Ownership of digital assets
  - Plans for business after death (continue or wind up)
  - New owners, if business continues
  - Arrangement for new ownership
- **Inheritance and Estate Taxes**
  - Applicable tax rates
    For inheritance tax? For estate taxes?
  - Provision for taxes
  - Threshold for inheritance taxes
  - Strategy for estate to save on inheritance and estate taxes
    - Using trusts
    - Using gifting
    - Inter vivos transfers
    - Other strategies

- **Life Insurance**
  - Current life insurance
  - Enough for the family to maintain their current lifestyle?
  - Enough to cover the immediate and short-term expenses?
  - Enough to cover the mortgage?
  - Are significant loans protected by life insurance?
  - Any scheduled review with a life insurance agent?
- **How are digital assets treated**
  - Discuss complete online portfolio
  - Decision on executor's access to digital assets
  - Will privacy be preserved?
  - Discuss a separate letter with passwords and online accounts
  - Impact of digital assets on tax liability

Having the necessary data and understanding of the process will ensure an informed discussion with the attorney or estate planner.

Always seek the advice of active and current professionals in their respective fields to ensure that all transactions will be legally correct.

9

I HAVE WRITTEN MY WILL. NOW WHAT?

"Carve your name on hearts, not tombstones. A legacy is etched into the minds of others and the stories they share about you."

Shannon L. Alder

Now that the will is completed, what happens next? The essential next steps are listed below:

DISCUSSION WITH EXECUTOR /PERSONAL REPRESENTATIVE

Meeting with the executor and getting their acceptance of the task is one of the first things to be done. Explaining the contents of the will makes their job more manageable and less stressful when it needs to get done. The executor/personal representative should receive a copy of the will.

STORAGE

There should be a current will in place, and the testator should always store it in a safe place. Persons who should know must be made aware of its existence and location. The testator should also keep all other relevant documents with the will.

KEEP WILL UPDATED

A will should be updated at least every three to five years or whenever there is a life change, whichever comes first. Life changes such as births, adoptions, marriages, divorces, remarriages, relocation, or deaths are reasons to have a new will written. Any changes in asset base, including purchase or sale of property, additional profits, losses, savings, income, or assets, also require a will review.

If persons are separated and not divorced, the spouse still benefits from the estate. Marriage negates an existing will. If a beneficiary predeceases the testator, the legacy left to them is brought back into the testator's estate, and an updated will should name a new beneficiary. If a new heir is not appointed, upon death, that asset will be treated under the rules of intestacy if there is no residuary clause. Any update in a will revokes the previous one, and, at probate, the original of the most current will is used.

KEEP RELATED DOCUMENTS UPDATED

All documents and instructions should be accessible to the executor. The testator should keep updating all the additional instruments prepared when writing their will. These vital instruments should also be stored with the will and be accessible to the executor. They include Trust, Codicil, Letter of Wishes, Power of Attorney, and Living Will, discussed in the following chapter.

REVOCATION

A will is ambulatory, meaning that a testator has the right to make as many changes to a will as needed during their lifetime. The requirements for writing a will need always to be in place. If there are many changes in updating one's will, one may choose to revoke it - rewrite it in its entirety. If the changes do not warrant a complete rewrite, a codicil may be an easy and cost-effective way to effect these changes.

WHAT IS A CODICIL?

This document is used to change an existing will when the testator does not wish to rewrite his will completely. Some reasons for writing a codicil might include changes in beneficiaries, the death of either the executor, trustee, or guardian, or property purchase or sale. These amendments should work in tandem with the original will.

Points to note in the writing of a codicil

Language
The preparer should write the codicil in the language in the same professional legal lingua and tone as the original will.

Identification
Putting a title to the codicil serves as identification, for example:
Codicil to the Last Will and Testament of ______________________________

Declaration
Its existence needs to be declared, linking it to the original will, for example:
"I____________________of______________________________________ in the City of
____________________, County of ____________________________
Country ____________________, being of sound mind, declare that this Codicil to the Last Will and Testament of ______________________________________ is effective on this date and shall hereby amend my Last Will and Testament dated as follows:"

Make amendments
For consistency, the changes to the will should be mentioned by matching the item number on the will, for example:
"Item 1 shall be amended to state ______________________________________"

An item may be completely deleted, for example:
"Item 2 shall be deleted"

An item may be added, for example:
"Item 10 is hereby added as follows: ____________________________________"

Reaffirm your wishes
A change in the codicil that contradicts the provisions of the will should be recorded, and a declaration made that it will overrule the wishes in the will, for example:
"Any statement in this Codicil to the Last Will and Testament of ____________________ of ____________________________________ that contradicts my Last Will and Testament dated ____________________ shall supersede my wishes in my Last Will and Testament"

Proofread
The codicil should be proofread to eliminate any errors.

Sign and Witness
A testator and two witnesses should sign and date the codicil. An attorney's preparation of the codicil will ensure accuracy and legal adherence in the respective area. This will also reduce the possibility of the will being contested. A will and a codicil should be stored together. If they get separated, the Court would only use the will's contents for probate. Sample Codicil *(Appendix 6)*.

SHOULD A WILL BE DISCUSSED WITH FAMILY?

Some persons discuss their wills with their family members, so they become more familiar with the terms. That makes it easier and less frustrating for them at the time of probate. Others prefer to make their family aware of a will, but they do not discuss the contents or the allocation. It is a personal choice.

CAN A WILL BE CONTESTED?

Any will can be contested in whole or in part. Family members, for example, a spouse, civil partner who has not remarried, an ex-spouse, a child, or someone who the testator maintained might contest their will.

A will might also be contested if there is any suspicion that the testator did not meet all the legal requirements when writing the will that is, being of legal age, being competent, of sound mind, and not acting under undue influence. A contested will could also result from any violation of local laws or an improper signature. A judge would need to pass a judgement on any contested will to settle the dispute.

A well-written will that meets all the qualifications reduces the possibility of a contest.

10 OTHER INSTRUMENTS FOR CONSIDERATION

"Someone is sitting in the shade today because someone planted a tree a long time ago."

Warren Buffett

When thinking about writing a will, it is an excellent time to "get your house in order" and consider the entire planning of your estate. A life insurance professional may be employed to review the testator's insurance portfolio, and an estate planner to organize the estate.

With "the magic of pen and paper and a few cents on the dollar," through life insurance, a legacy can instantly be created and left for one's beneficiaries. It might otherwise be difficult or improbable to accumulate that legacy during one's lifetime. With the introduction of technology in the application process, the "magic" can be created even faster.

The estate planner's recommendations might include Trusts, Power of Attorney, Living Will, and a Letter of Wishes. Each is discussed below.

LIFE INSURANCE

Life insurance plays a significant role in estate planning. Naming a beneficiary enables the proceeds after death to be passed directly to the named beneficiary without a will, thus speeding up the asset transfer.

A life insurance policy can be an asset to provide needed cash for the continuity of living expenses, clearing outstanding taxes, mortgages, and administrative fees, and preventing the forced sale of a property.

HERE'S HOW IT WORKS:

In addition to the ability to pay, depending on the type of insurance, a life insurance company will consider other factors before accepting an applicant's risk and approving an application for life insurance.

Following an application, the company's underwriter considers the applicant's level of risk to the company and determines the acceptability of that risk and the price or ***premium*** to charge. Some factors include age, gender, health, employment, financial position, and lifestyle. The underwriter, therefore, considers the health conditions; the risk level of the applicant's occupation, for example, aircraft pilot, underground miner, and logger; the applicant's income and credit score; hazardous lifestyle activities such as scuba diving, race car driving, bungee jumping or parasailing. Driving record and credit score may also help determine one's level of responsibility and could factor in determining the premium. If a risk is considered high to the company, the underwriter may refuse to accept the application, or it may offer it at a higher rate, termed a ***rating***.

Persons with excellent health who are nonsmokers and pass the other tests could get ***preferred rates*** below the standard premium. Premiums are generally more competitive for younger ages and females as they have a lower mortality rate.

Some larger-sized applications require a medical examination. However, there are ***guaranteed issued*** policies for which there is no medical requirement with little or no underwriting. These usually offer limited coverage to a maximum of thirty thousand (US$30,000) or forty thousand (US$40,000). On death, the policy proceeds are paid tax-free to the named beneficiary or beneficiaries, unless death is by suicide within two years of issue or if murder is involved and the beneficiary/beneficiaries are held responsible.

Life insurance can be used to cover different needs; chief among them are income protection, mortgage or loan protection, final expenses, and business. An insurance consultant will be able to assist with identifying the testator's needs and recommend the appropriate solution.

IS LIFE INSURANCE A NECESSITY?

Life insurance creates sizable estates, provides financial stability in one's estate, and relieves the emotional and financial stress that beneficiaries could experience after the death of their breadwinner. They need to meet short-term and more immediate expenses, pull the pieces together and move on with their lives.

Life insurance allows beneficiaries to maintain their lifestyle, pays for children's education, pays off mortgages, provides for the continuation of businesses, and leaves legacies for future generations.

Most life insurance companies provide excellent customer service. They are efficient in the speedy settlement of death claims, especially for policies with named beneficiaries. A professional life insurance agent can assess one's assets, liabilities, goals, and aspirations to uncover financial needs and advise on the amount and type of life insurance needed.

Should life insurance be included in one's portfolio? The testator must decide.

TRUSTS

PARTIES TO A TRUST

Trustor

The trustor, otherwise called the grantor, settlor, or trust maker, is the person who owns the asset, transfers its ownership into a trust, and creates an agreement for transfer to the beneficiary based on the agreed terms.

Trustee

The person or entity responsible for managing the asset established by the trustor and paying out the proceeds to the named beneficiary or beneficiaries based on the agreement is the trustee.

Beneficiary

The beneficiary is the person, persons, or entity that receives the asset from the trustor via the trustee, based on the agreement.

TRUST

A trust is a fiduciary arrangement where a trustee holds a trustor's assets and distributes those assets to the beneficiary according to the trustor's wishes. Funds transferred into the trust are no longer owned by the trustor.

ETCHED IN MY MEMORY

My first death claim as a Life Insurance Salesperson

Kevin was 27 years old, vibrant, intelligent, and had his whole life ahead of him. I was excited for him when he introduced me to the love of his life, his fiancé Maggie. Shortly after that, they were married and went on their honeymoon on Jamaica's north coast. Two days later, I got a call that he was ill, something I found hard to believe. Yes, he had dived into the swimming pool, and something terrible happened. His entire body changed color. He was airlifted into Kingston and hospitalized.

I rushed to visit him and quickly asked if he wanted to change his will. He did! I quickly wrote a new will by hand, had him sign it, then rushed to see an attorney to have it typed and prepared for his signature. Two hours later, the attorney and I returned to visit Kevin with a typewritten will reflecting his wishes. As I proudly told him we had everything done for him and just needed his signature, he said,
"Gloria, is that you?"
I asked, "What do you mean?"
Kevin was blind!!

He was diagnosed with an exceedingly rare and aggressive type of cancer, and the only thing that could have saved his life was a blood transfusion, but he could not take one because of his religious belief.

I watched as family members rushed in to share his last moments with him. More family members and friends visited the following day, some journeying from hours away.

I got the job done, but my heart could not take the pain, so I left and awaited the call that he had passed. It came two days later!

I shall never forget this incident in my lifetime!

The moral of this story is that we never know when we will die. Some die young, even when they seem to be in excellent health; some live to a ripe old age. Once an adult, you should organize your estate!

Trusts ensure continued support for a beneficiary, most popularly for minors and disabled children. They are beneficial for providing care for disabled minors whose arrangements might go beyond the age of minority. Funds are sometimes left in a trust for a child's education, with specific rules to control expenditure for the intended purpose. Usually, amounts are made in installments and over time, rather than a single payment. This feature is also effective for curbing excessive spending by a considered financially irresponsible beneficiary.

Several other reasons exist for establishing a trust, including legal protection of the assets in the trust, protection against creditors, and ensuring that the trustee distributes the assets according to the trustor's wishes. As these assets have named beneficiaries, they fall outside of the will, avoid probate, save time and court fees, and sometimes are not considered part of one's estate, thus reducing the value of the assets and the taxes on the testator's estate.

One should name a corporation or at least two persons to ensure continuity in the event of the death of one of the trustees. The main cost of establishing a trust is the expense of having it set up by an attorney or estate planner.

There are different types of Trusts:

LIVING TRUST

Sometimes called "inter vivos" or revocable trust, a living trust passes property and avoids costs and delays at probate. It is created and goes into effect during the trustor's lifetime. As the name suggests, the trustor may change his beneficiary as often as he wishes during his lifetime with revocable trusts. He may even move the assets in and out of the trust as he desires. The trustor still owns the assets in a revocable living trust forming a part of his estate, making him liable for applicable taxes. On the trustor's death, a revocable living trust automatically becomes an irrevocable trust.

IRREVOCABLE TRUST

In an irrevocable trust, the testator may not change the beneficiary. The trustor would have handed over the ownership of the assets to the trustee, which lowers his asset base and hence his tax liability.

TESTAMENTARY TRUST

A testamentary trust goes into effect after the trust maker dies. The trust maker names the trust as the beneficiary, and the executor forms the testamentary trust on their death, based on the stipulations of the will.

This act moves the property into the trust on the trust maker's death and is one way of avoiding time-consuming and costly probate.

POWER OF ATTORNEY

Another document to be considered during estate planning is a Power of Attorney. In this document, authority is given to someone else to make decisions on their behalf when they cannot make them for themselves. Some covered areas include finances, healthcare, medical treatment, and lifestyle.

One can use a revocable living trust in place of a Power of Attorney. *Appendix 3* shows a Durable Financial Power of Attorney. A Living Will may be used as a Power of Attorney on medical matters. A Power of Attorney becomes void at death.

LIVING WILLS

People have different thoughts about the quality of life they would like to enjoy in their final days. A Living Will is used to give directives regarding one's preferences for medical treatment if they cannot communicate them independently. It is a written legal document that legally authorizes an appointed individual to make decisions on their behalf based on the wishes outlined therein. It eliminates persons making decisions on one's behalf that would be against their desires.

It is best to record one's wishes regarding preferred medical treatments for staying alive and other medical decisions, such as pain management or organ donation. Without directives and with the best intentions, family members may elect medical treatment that may not be in keeping with one's preferences. An example would be keeping an individual on a ventilator if they cannot breathe independently or being fed through a feeding tube for an extended period when they might have elected to die naturally rather than have their life extended medically.

This document should be completed by all adults as they could need it if they become too ill to communicate their wishes, for example, while in a coma or the late stages of dementia. *(Appendix 4).*

LETTER OF WISHES

When writing one's will, one may also wish to prepare a Letter of Wishes to supplement the will. This separate document is beneficial as a guide but is not legally binding. In the letter, the testator gives the executor and the trustee specific instructions on how they would like them to exercise their powers. It is vital when the executor and trustee have broad control. A Letter of Wishes can pass on assets that, although they might have monetary value, have sentimental value, such as jewelry and furniture.

A will should list assets with monetary value and name their beneficiaries. The testator might use a Letter of Wishes to explain a decision documented in the will, which might otherwise cause friction in the family. It could also demonstrate intent in the event a will is contested. A sample of a Letter of Wishes is in *Appendix 5.*

ETCHED IN MY MEMORY

Trust

Fred established a trust for his son, payable in tranches at ages sixteen, twenty-one, twenty-five, and thirty. He was able to send himself to college, buy a car, make a down payment on an apartment and have a hefty savings account.

Gifts like these are never forgotten and ensure that the trust maker's legacy continues.

11 THE TIME IS NOW!

"Outlive your life!"

Max Lucado

Planning one's estate is not only for persons advanced in age but for everyone from the age of majority. Although this might seem like "preaching to the choir," the importance of having a will cannot be overemphasized. It provides the opportunity to record one's wishes for the orderly distribution of their estate to their selected beneficiaries.

There is urgency in planning one's estate and writing a will, whatever the size. A will is a special gift to one's heirs, a legacy that alleviates stress and confusion after the testator's death. One should never think that they do not own enough to make a will. Most persons own something, plus, in reiterating, "through the miracle of pen and paper and with a few pennies on the dollar," life insurance helps in a big way to provide a substantial legacy almost immediately. People forget about their mortality sometimes. They are reminded of it once a loved one has a recent death, but, indeed, it should always be remembered.

In 2021 between fifty percent (50%) and sixty percent (60%) of Americans did not have a will or had not done their estate planning. In Jamaica, the latest figures show that the Office of the Administrator-General manages assets and cash valued at approximately twelve billion dollars (J$12 billion) / (US$80 million) for persons who had children and died intestate.

Insurance agents have experienced both the positive and negative aspects of life insurance. They do not forget the negative ones, those failed attempts where despite their efforts, they were unsuccessful in getting persons to adequately prepare for their families after their deaths. They sometimes reflect on their relationship with the deceased before death, the convincing, the procrastination, and the agreements. Some prospects wish they had heeded the agents' advice and had implemented their recommendations.

Procrastination affects goals and dreams; it affects families and businesses. It is painful to witness the hardship caused when there is not enough in an estate to take care of the future needs of a family. It pains, even more, when there is enough in the estate, but there is no will, forcing families to wait, sometimes for years, to receive their legacies.

Dying testate or intestate is a decision for every individual to make. Will they die knowing they had done their best to provide for their families and have their legacies live on, or will they cause lack and confusion for their families after death? Having the information and knowing the advantages of estate planning, each individual has the opportunity to get it done and have the final say regarding the distribution of their estate to their beneficiaries.

Everyone needs to prepare for tomorrow, so why not start today? Deciding to create or update one's portfolio should include incorporating the additional financial instruments discussed, which will help structure an estate. Early planning can also be beneficial as some things cost less at a younger age.

It is hoped that the shared information, experiences, and tips will sufficiently motivate each person to get this vital matter taken care of today. Having one's estate organized for their family is a noble thing. It is essential. It is critical. It needs to get done.

Now is the time to ask:

- Do I have a will?
- Is it current?
- Has my financial or personal situation changed?
- Are there changes I would like to make to my existing will?
- Is there a new family addition?
- Is there a new business?
- Do I have additional assets?
- Do I know where all my titles and other documents are?
- Why don't I do my estate planning now?

Do yourself a favor. If you have no will, get one done today. If you have one, does it need to be updated? If so, do it now.

Each person needs to decide on the legacy they will leave for their family and future generations. Remember, the consequences of dying without a will far exceed the time to write one!

Treat it not as something that you should do but as something you MUST do!

THE TIME IS NOW!

ETCHED IN MY MEMORY

Don't procrastinate

Glen Jones was born into an impoverished family. He promised himself that he would work as hard as needed to lift his mother and siblings out of poverty. He lived up to his promise, did well in school, and received a scholarship to high school. Seeing an opportunity, he got involved in sports and won a track scholarship to university.

Glen remained the breadwinner of his family. After working for many years, he opened his own business, naming his mother as his partner, and soon the potential became evident. During this time, a life insurance agent discussed his portfolio to protect his family and business and have his will written. He decided he would wait a while.

Shortly after meeting Gina, they started making plans to marry in a year. They worked together in the business, and it began to grow. They agreed that as soon as they could afford it, they would first purchase a home for his mother and siblings, and Gina would become a part-owner of the business. The insurance agent kept in touch with them, but he kept procrastinating.

One day he was returning home from a business meeting, met in a terrible accident with an oncoming truck, and was rushed to the hospital. The life insurance agent visited him in hospital, but he was unconscious and died shortly after. That shattered his plans - he did not get a chance to marry Gina, purchase a home for his family, purchase life insurance to leave tax-free dollars for his family, write a will or make Gina a part-owner of the business.

The business had potential, but it did not have enough to assist his family significantly. Although Gina tried to keep it afloat, it suffered after Glen's death. His family waited for just under three years to receive the little he left, and Gina did not inherit the business as Glen's mother still owned it.

Procrastination is not just the thief of time; it also steals dreams and aspirations.

Don't procrastinate! Get it done today!

THIS IS THE LAST WILL AND TESTAMENT

Of me ____

of ____

in the parish of ____

I hereby revoke all wills and testamentary dispositions previously made by me and declare this to be my last Will and Testament.

I appoint ______________________ of ______________________

and ______________________ of ______________________

to be the Executors and Trustees of this my Will, and Trustees for all the purposes of the Settled Land and Conveyance Laws. I direct my Executors and Trustees to pay my just debts and funeral and Testamentary Expenses.

I give, bequeath and devise

All the rest and residue of my estate I give to

IN WITNESS whereof I have set my hand to this my Last Will and Testament

This ______________________ day of ______________________

(Testator to sign here) ____

(Witnesses to sign here)

Name: ______________	Name: ______________
Address: ______________	Address: ______________
Occupation: ______________	Occupation: ______________

Florida Last Will and Testament
of

____

Pursuant to Chapter 732 (Probate Code: Intestate Succession and Wills)

I, ________________________, resident in the City of ____________________, County of ____________________, State of Florida being of sound mind, not acting under duress or undue influence, and fully understanding the nature and extent of all my property and of this disposition thereof, do hereby make, publish, and declare this document to be my Last Will and Testament, and hereby revoke any and all other wills and codicils heretofore made by me.

I. EXPENSES & TAXES

I direct that all my debts, and expenses of my last illness, funeral, and burial, be paid as soon after my death as may be reasonably convenient, and I hereby authorize my Personal Representative, hereinafter appointed, to settle and discharge, in his or her absolute discretion, any claims made against my estate.

I further direct that my Personal Representative shall pay out of my estate any and all estate and inheritance taxes payable by reason of my death in respect of all items included in the computation of such taxes, whether passing under this Will or otherwise. Said taxes shall be paid by my Personal Representative as if such taxes were my debts without recovery of any part of such tax payments from anyone who receives any item included in such computation.

II. PERSONAL REPRESENTATIVE

I nominate and appoint ________________________, of ____________________________, County of _________________________, State of ____________________________ as Personal Representative of my estate and I request that (he/she) be appointed temporary Personal Representative if (he/she) applies. If my Personal Representative fails or ceases to so serve, then I nominate ____________________________of ___________________________, County of ____________________________, State of _______________________ to serve.

III. DISPOSITION OF PROPERTY

I devise and bequeath my property, both real and personal and wherever situated, as follows:

1st Beneficiary

_________________________ [full name], currently of _________________________ [address], as my _________________________ [relation] whose last four (4) digits of their Social Security Number (SSN) are xxx-xx-_____ with the following property:

2nd Beneficiary

________________________ [full name], currently of ________________________ [address], as my ________________________ [relation] whose last four (4) digits of their Social Security Number (SSN) are xxx-xx-_____ with the following property:

____

3rd Beneficiary

________________________ [full name], currently of ________________________ [address], as my ________________________ [relation] whose last four (4) digits of their Social Security Number (SSN) are xxx-xx-_____ with the following property:

____

If any of my beneficiaries have pre-deceased me, then any property that they would have received if they had not pre-deceased me shall be distributed in equal shares to the remaining beneficiaries.

If any of my property cannot be readily sold and distributed, then it may be donated to any charitable organization or organizations of my Personal Representative's choice. If any property cannot be readily sold or donated, my Personal Representative may, without liability, dispose of such property as my Personal Representative may deem appropriate. I authorize my Personal Representative to pay as an administration expense of my estate the expense of selling, advertising for sale, packing, shipping, insuring and delivering such property.

IV. OMISSION

Except to the extent that I have included them in this Will, I have intentionally, and not as a result of any mistake or inadvertence, omitted in this Will to provide for any family members and/or issue of mine, if any, however defined by law, presently living or hereafter born or adopted.

V. BOND

No bond shall be required of any fiduciary serving hereunder, whether or not specifically named in this Will, or if a bond is required by law, then no surety will be required on such bond.

VI. DISCRETIONARY POWERS OF PERSONAL REPRESENTATIVE

My Personal Representative, shall have and may exercise the following discretionary powers in addition to any common law or statutory powers without the necessity of court license or approval:

A. To retain for whatever period my Personal Representative deems advisable any property, including property owned by me at my death, and to invest and reinvest in any property, both real and personal, regardless of whether any particular investment would be proper for a Personal Representative and regardless of the extent of diversification of the assets held hereunder.

B. To sell and to grant options to purchase all or any part of my estate, both real and personal, at any time, at public or private sale, for consideration, whether or not the highest possible consideration, and upon terms, including credit, as my Personal Representative deems advisable, and to execute, acknowledge, and deliver deeds or other instruments in connection therewith.

C. To lease any real estate for terms and conditions as my Personal Representative deems advisable, including the granting of options to renew, options to extend the term or terms, and options to purchase.

D. To pay, compromise, settle or otherwise adjust any claims, including taxes, asserted in favor of or against me, my estate or my Personal Representative.

E. To make any separation into shares in whole or in part in kind and at values determined by my Personal Representative, with or without regard to tax basis, and to allocate different kinds and disproportionate amounts of property and undivided interests in property among the shares.

F. To make such elections under the tax laws as my Personal Representative shall deem appropriate, including elections with respect to qualified terminable interest property, exemptions and the use of deductions as income tax or estate tax deductions, and to determine whether to make any adjustments between income and principal on account of any election so made.

G. To make any elections permitted under any pension, profit sharing, employee stock ownership or other benefit plan.

H. To employ others in connection with the administration of my estate, including legal counsel, investment advisors, brokers, accountants and agents and to pay reasonable compensation in addition to my Personal Representative's compensation.

I. To vote any shares of stock or other securities in person or by proxy; to assert or waive any stockholder's rights or privilege to subscribe for or otherwise acquire additional stock; to deposit securities in any voting trust or with any committee.

J. To borrow and to pledge or mortgage any property as collateral, and to make secured or unsecured loans. My Personal Representative is specifically authorized to make loans without interest to any beneficiary hereunder. No individual or entity loaning property to my Personal Representative or trustee shall be held to see to the application of such property.

K. My Personal Representative shall also in his or her absolute discretion determine the allocation of any GST exemption available to me at my death to property passing under this Will or otherwise. The determination of my Personal Representative with respect to any elections or allocation, if made or taken in good faith, shall be binding upon all affected.

VII. CONTESTING BENEFICIARY

If any beneficiary under this Will, or any trust herein mentioned, contests or attacks this Will or any of its provisions, any share or interest in my estate given to that contesting beneficiary under this Will is revoked and shall be disposed of in the same manner provided herein as if that contesting beneficiary had predeceased me.

VIII. GUARDIAN AD LITEM NOT REQUIRED

I direct that the representation by a guardian ad litem of the interests of persons unborn, unascertained or legally incompetent to act in proceedings for the allowance of accounts hereunder be dispensed with to the extent permitted by law.

IX. GENDER

Whenever the context permits, the term "Personal Representative" shall include "Executor" and "Administrator," the use of a particular gender shall include any other gender, and references to the singular or the plural shall be interchangeable. All references to the Internal Revenue Code shall mean the Internal Revenue Code of 1986 or any successor Code. All references to estate taxes shall include inheritance and other death taxes.

X. ASSIGNMENT

The interest of any beneficiary in this Will, shall not be alienable, assignable, attachable, transferable nor paid by way of anticipation, nor in compliance with any order, assignment or covenant and shall not be applied to, or held liable for, any of their debts or obligations either in law or equity and shall not in any event pass to his, her, or their assignee under any instrument or under any insolvency or bankruptcy law, and shall not be subject to the interference or control of creditors, spouses or others.

XI. GOVERNING LAW

This document shall be governed by the laws in the State of Florida.

XII. BINDING ARRANGEMENT

Any decision by my Personal Representative with respect to any discretionary power hereunder shall be final and binding on all persons interested. Unless due to my Executor's own willful default or gross negligence, no Executor shall be liable for said Executor's acts or omissions or those of any co-Executor or prior Executor.

I, the undersigned ______________________, do hereby declare that I sign and execute this instrument as my last Will, that I sign it willingly in the presence of each of the undersigned witnesses, and that I execute it as my free and voluntary act for the purposes herein expressed, on this ____ day of ________________, 20____.

______________________________ Testator Signature

______________________________ Testator (Printed Name)

The foregoing instrument, was on this ____ day of ________________, 20____, subscribed on each page and at the end thereof by ________________________, the above-named Testator, and by (him/her) signed, sealed, published and declared to be (his/her) LAST WILL AND TESTAMENT, in the presence of us and each of us, who thereupon, at (his/her) request, in (his/her) presence, and in the presence of each other, have hereunto subscribed our names as attesting witnesses thereto.

____________________________ ______________________________
Witness Signature Address

____________________________ ______________________________
Witness Signature Address

TESTAMENTARY AFFIDAVIT

STATE OF ____________________

COUNTY OF __________________, SS.

Before me, the undersigned authority, on this day personally appeared ___________, testator, ____________________, witness and ___________________, witness, known to me to be the testator and the witnesses, respectively, whose names are signed to the attached or foregoing instrument, and, all of these persons being by me duly sworn, the testator declared to me and to the witnesses in my presence that the instrument is the testator's last will and that the testator has willingly signed or directed another to sign for him/her, and that the testator executed it as the testator's free and voluntary act for the purposes therein expressed; and each of the witnesses stated to me, in the presence of the testator, that they signed the will as witnesses and that to the best of their knowledge the testator was eighteen (18) years of age or over, of sound mind and under no constraint or undue influence.

____________________________ ____________________________
Testator Signature Witness Signature

____
Witness Signature

Subscribed and sworn to before me by the said testator and the said witnesses, this

____ day of ________________, 20____.

____
Notary Public

My Commission expires:

DURABLE FINANCIAL POWER OF ATTORNEY

On the ___ day of __________________, 20____ I, __________________, the principal, of __________________, State of __________________, hereby designate __________________, of __________________, State of __________________, my attorney-in-fact (hereinafter my "attorney-in-fact"), to act as initialed below, in my name, in my stead and for my benefit, hereby revoking any and all financial powers of attorney I may have executed in the past.

EFFECTIVE DATE

(Choose the applicable paragraph by placing your initials in the preceding space)

________ - A. I grant my attorney-in-fact the powers set forth herein immediately upon the execution of this document. These powers shall not be affected by any subsequent disability or incapacity I may experience in the future.

or

________ - B. I grant my attorney-in-fact the powers set forth herein only when it has been determined in writing, by my attending physician, that I am unable to properly handle my financial affairs.

POWERS OF ATTORNEY-IN-FACT

My attorney-in-fact shall exercise powers in my best interests and for my welfare, as a fiduciary. My attorney-in-fact shall have the following powers:

(Choose the applicable power(s) by placing your initials in the preceding space)

________ **BANKING** - To receive and deposit funds in any financial institution, and to withdraw funds by check or otherwise to pay for goods, services, and any other personal and business expenses for my benefit. If necessary to effect my attorney-in-fact's powers, my attorney-in-fact is authorized to execute any document required to be signed by such banking institution.

________ **SAFE DEPOSIT BOX** - To have access at any time or times to any safe-deposit box rented by me or to which I may have access, wheresoever located, including drilling, if necessary, and to remove all or any part of the contents thereof, and to surrender or relinquish said safe-deposit box; and any institution in which any such safe-deposit box may be located shall not incur any liability to me or my estate as a result of permitting my attorney-in-fact to exercise this power.

________ **LENDING OR BORROWING** - To make loans in my name; to borrow money in my name, individually or jointly with others; to give promissory notes or other obligations therefor; and to deposit or mortgage as collateral or for security for the payment thereof any or all of my securities, real estate, personal property, or other property of whatever nature and wherever situated, held by me personally or in trust for my benefit.

________ **GOVERNMENT BENEFITS** - To apply for and receive any government benefits for which I may be eligible or become eligible, including but not limited to, Social Security, Medicare and Medicaid.

________ **RETIREMENT PLAN** - To contribute to, select payment option of, roll-over, and receive benefits of any retirement plan or IRA I may own, except my attorney-in-fact shall not have power to change the beneficiary of any of my retirement plans or IRAs.

________ **TAXES** - To complete and sign any local, state and federal tax returns on my behalf, pay any taxes and assessments due and receive credits and refunds owed to me and to sign any tax agency documents necessary to effectuate these powers.

________ **INSURANCE** - To purchase, pay premiums and make claims on life, health, automobile and homeowners' insurance on my behalf, except my attorney-in-fact shall not have the power to cash in or change the beneficiary of any life insurance policy.

________ **REAL ESTATE** - To acquire, purchase, exchange, lease, grant options to sell, and sell and convey real property, or any interests therein, on such terms and conditions, including credit arrangements, as my attorney-in-fact shall deem proper; to execute, acknowledge and deliver, under seal or otherwise, any and all assignments, transfers, deeds, papers, documents or instruments which my attorney-in-fact shall deem necessary in connection therewith.

________ **PERSONAL PROPERTY** - To acquire, purchase, exchange, lease, grant options to sell, and sell and convey personal property, or any interests therein, on such terms and conditions, including credit arrangements, as my attorney-in-fact shall deem proper; to execute, acknowledge and deliver, under seal or otherwise, any and all assignments, transfers, titles, papers, documents or instruments which my attorney-in-fact shall deem necessary in connection therewith; to purchase, sell or otherwise dispose of, assign, transfer and convey shares of stock, bonds, securities and other personal property now or hereafter belonging to me, whether standing in my name or otherwise, and wherever situated.

________ **POWER TO MANAGE PROPERTY**- To maintain, repair, improve, invest, manage, insure, rent, lease, encumber, and in any manner deal with any real or personal property, tangible or intangible, or any interests therein, that I now own or may hereafter acquire, in my name and for my benefit, upon such terms and conditions as my attorney-in-fact shall deem proper.

_________ **GIFTS** - To make gifts, grants, or other transfers (including the forgiveness of indebtedness and the completion of any charitable pledges I may have made) without consideration, either outright or in trust to such person(s) (including my attorney-in-fact hereunder) or organizations as my attorney-in-fact shall select, including, without limitation, the following actions: (a) transfer by gift in advancement of a bequest or devise to beneficiaries under my will or in the absence of a will to my spouse and descendants in whatever degree; and (b) release of any life interest, or waiver, renunciation, disclaimer, or declination of any gift to me by will, deed, or trust

________ **LEGAL ADVICE AND PROCEEDINGS** - To obtain and pay for legal advice, to initiate or defend legal and administrative proceedings on my behalf, including actions against third parties who refuse, without cause, to honor this instrument.

SPECIAL INSTRUCTIONS: On the following lines are any special instructions limiting or extending the powers I give to my attorney-in-fact (Write "None" if no additional instructions are given):

____

____

____

____

AUTHORITY OF ATTORNEY-IN-FACT: Any party dealing with my attorney-in-fact hereunder may rely absolutely on the authority granted herein and need not look to the application of any proceeds nor the authority of my attorney-in-fact as to any action taken hereunder. In this regard, no person who may in good faith act in reliance upon the representations of my attorney-in-fact or the authority granted hereunder shall incur any liability to me or my estate as a result of such act. I hereby ratify and confirm whatever my attorney-in-fact shall lawfully do under this instrument. My attorney-in-fact is authorized as he or she deems necessary to bring an action in court so that this instrument shall be given the full power and effect that I intend on by executing it.

LIABILITY OF ATTORNEY-IN-FACT: My attorney-in-fact shall not incur any liability to me under this power except for a breach of fiduciary duty.

REIMBURSEMENT OF ATTORNEY-IN-FACT: My attorney-in-fact is entitled to reimbursement for reasonable expenses incurred in exercising powers hereunder, and to reasonable compensation for services provided as attorney-in-fact.

AMENDMENT AND REVOCATION: I can amend or revoke this power of attorney through a writing delivered to my attorney-in-fact. Any amendment or revocation is ineffective as to a third party until such third party has notice of such revocation or amendment.

STATE LAW: This Power of Attorney is governed by the laws of the State of ______________________.

PHOTOCOPIES: Photocopies of this document can be relied upon as though they were originals.

IN WITNESS WHEREOF, I have on this ____ day of __________________, 20____, executed this Financial Power of Attorney.

____

Principal's Signature

We, the witnesses, each do hereby declare in the presence of the principal that the principal signed and executed this instrument in the presence of each of us, that the principal signed it willingly, that each of us hereby signs this Power of Attorney as witness at the request of the principal and in the principal's presence, and that, to the best of our knowledge, the principal is eighteen years of age or over, of sound mind, and under no constraint or undue influence.

____

Witness's Signature

____

Address

____

Witness's Signature

____

Address

STATE OF __________________

__________________ County, ss.

On this ____ day of _________________, 20____, before me appeared __________________, as Principal of this Power of Attorney who proved to me through government issued photo identification to be the above-named person, in my presence executed foregoing instrument and acknowledged that (s)he executed the same as his/her free act and deed.

____

Notary Public

My commission expires: ___________

SPECIMEN SIGNATURE AND ACCEPTANCE OF APPOINTMENT

I, ____________________, the attorney-in-fact named above, hereby accept appointment as attorney-in-fact in accordance with the foregoing instrument.

____

Attorney-in-Fact's Signature

STATE OF __________________

__________________ County, ss.

On this ____ day of __________________, 20____, before me appeared ____________________, as Attorney-in-Fact of this Power of Attorney who proved to me through government issued photo identification to be the above-named person, in my presence executed the foregoing acceptance of appointment and acknowledged that (s)he executed the same as his/her free act and deed.

____

Notary Public

My commission expires: ___________

LIVING WILL (DECLARATION)

This document contains two parts. Both parts are for use when you can no longer communicate your health care wishes to your doctors. You may choose to sign one or the other or both.

The first form is called a Health Care Directive, also known as a living will. The Health Care Directive allows you to tell your health care providers your preferences for end of life treatment.

The second form is called a Health Care Power of Attorney. This Health Care Power of Attorney allows you to appoint another person to make health care decisions on your behalf taking into account your wishes.

This form was completed and signed on ________________, 20____.

I. HEALTH CARE DIRECTIVE (LIVING WILL)

(If you do not wish to fill out this form and just wish to designate a health care agent, draw an "X" through the following section)

I, ______________________, with a mailing address of ______________________, with the last four (4) digits of my social security number (SSN) being xxx-xx-_______ (Hereinafter may be referred to as the 'Principal') desire to advise my doctors and medical providers of my wishes for my health care in the event I am not able to communicate my wishes.

A. LIFE SUPPORT

I desire that my doctor make a concerted effort to return me to an acceptable quality of life using then available treatments and therapies. However, if my quality of life becomes unacceptable as I have defined below and my doctors have determined that my condition will not improve (is irreversible), I direct that all treatments that extend my life be withdrawn.

An unacceptable quality of life means (initial and check all that apply):

______ ☐ - Chronic coma or persistent vegetative state
______ ☐ - No longer able to communicate my needs
______ ☐ - No longer able to recognize family or friends
______ ☐ - Total dependence on others for daily care
______ ☐ - Other: ____.

(initial and check one)

______ ☐ - Even if I have the quality of life described above, I still wish to be treated with food and water by tube or intravenously (IV).
______ ☐ - If I have the quality of life described above, I do NOT wish to be treated with food and water by tube or intravenously (IV).

B. CERTAIN LIFE-SUSTAINING TREATMENT: (You do not have to initial and check any of these if you do not wish to)

Some people do not wish to have certain life sustaining treatments under any circumstance, even if recovery is a possibility. Check treatments below, if any, that you do not wish to have under any circumstances (initial and check all that apply):

______ ☐ - Cardiopulmonary Resuscitation (CPR)
______ ☐ - Ventilation (breathing machine)
______ ☐ - Feeding tube
______ ☐ - Dialysis
______ ☐ - Other: ____.

C. END OF LIFE WISHES (hospice care, funeral arrangements, etc.):

When I am near death, it is important to me that:
____
____
____
____

II. HEALTH CARE (MEDICAL) POWER OF ATTORNEY WITH MENTAL HEALTH AUTHORITY

It provides peace of mind to be able to choose someone you know and who knows you to make healthcare decisions on your behalf when you no longer can communicate your wishes. It is important that you discuss your wishes with your health care agent so they can be sure to make sure your wishes are carried out by the health care providers. If you DO NOT, however, choose someone to make decisions for you, write NONE in the line for the agent's name.

I, ______________________, as Principal, designate ______________________, as my agent to act in all matters relating to my health care (including my mental health care) and including, without limitation, the power to give or refuse consent to all medical and surgical treatments, hospitalizations and related health care. This power of attorney is effective at the point when I am not longer able to communicate my health care wishes. My agent's decisions under this power of attorney, during any period when I am unable to make and/or communicate my health care decisions or when there is uncertainty as to whether I am dead or alive, are binding on my heirs, devisees and personal representatives.

My agent's address and phone number are as follows:

Phone: ______________________________
Address: ______________________________

(initial and check all that apply)

______ ☐ - I specifically consent to giving my agent the power to admit me to an inpatient or partial psychiatric hospitalization program if ordered by my physician. (Initial if this is your choice)
______ ☐ - This Health Care Directive including Mental Health Care Power of Attorney may not be revoked if I am incapacitated. (Initial if this is your choice)

If my agent is unwilling or unable to serve, I hereby appoint as my successor agent:

Successor Agent's Name: ______________________________
Phone: ______________________________
Address: ______________________________

I intend for my agent to receive any and all of my health records and information as if I were the one requesting such information. This release authority applies to any information governed by the Health Insurance Portability and Accountability Act of 1996 (aka HIPAA), 42 USC 1420D and 45 CFR 160-164.

I have signed this document on this ________________, 20____.

Principal's Signature: ______________________________
Print Name: ______________________________

You may either choose two (2) witnesses and/or a notary to acknowledge your signature.

WITNESS ACKNOWLEDGMENT

On the date set forth above, I hereby state as follows:

The above named person is personally known to me, and I believe him/her to be of sound mind and to have voluntarily executed this document. I am at least 18 years old, not related to him/her by blood, marriage or adoption, and I am not an agent or successor agent named in this document. To my knowledge, I am not a beneficiary of his/her will or any codicil, and I have no claim against his/her estate. I am not directly involved in his/her health care.

Witness 1

Witness 1 Signature: ______________________________
Print Name: ______________________________
Phone: ______________________________
Address: ______________________________

Witness 2

Witness 2 Signature: ______________________________
Print Name: ______________________________
Phone: ______________________________
Address: ______________________________

NOTARY ACKNOWLEDGMENT

State of _____________ }
County of _____________ }

Signed and sworn to me on the ___ day of __________________, in the year 20___.

I, the undersigned authority in and for said County in said State, hereby certify that the

Principal __________________, whose name is signed above in this living will, and who is known to me, acknowledged before me on this day that, being informed of the contents of the said document, (s)he executed the same voluntarily on the day the same bears date.

Given under my hand this _____________, 20____.

Notary Public Signature ____________________
Printed Name: ______________________________.
My commission expires: _____________________

(Notary Seal)

XYZ Estate

Address

Address

Date

Dear Executors of XYZ Estate,

I would firstly like to thank all my family and friends for all the love and care expressed to me, especially in my final days. I sincerely appreciate everything you did for me. To my executors, whereas I understand that I cannot dictate how you operate in probating my will, and whereas I have every confidence that you will handle my wishes to the best of your abilities, I would like to add this letter as a guide for consideration. My assets and my wishes are listed below:

Property: In selling my property, I am requesting that you try to get the best price you possibly can. I have made other arrangements in my will for my children, John and Jane, to whom the proceeds from the sale are willed, that they will be able to wait on the sale for the best price

My business: As you know, my business was doing well financially, and I specialized in providing the best customer service for my clients. John studied business and would surely be able to take the business to the next level but, over the years, Jane has worked tirelessly in the business and understands the way we do things. I know Joan loves flowers and knows our customers well. Additionally, her personality will help to keep and increase our customer base. I chose her because I feel that maintenance of our high level of customer service will drive the future success of the business. I do not wish for John to be upset in any way, but I feel that he might wish to pursue a business in something other than flowers. That explains why I left a larger portion of cash for him to enable him to start a business of his own.

Personal Belongings: For all my personal belongings that will be kept, I know there will be no problem in dividing them based on the tastes of my family members. Feel free to take what you genuinely like.

I love you all,

Mary

CODICIL TO WILL OF

____

I, ____________________, with a mailing address of ____________________ City of ____________________, State of ____________________ ("Testator") create this Codicil to my Last Will dated the ____ day of ____________________, 20____ ("Last Will"). I hereby republish and declare said Last Will as amended by this Codicil to be my Last Will.

I. Declaration. I hereby declare the following amendments in this Codicil:

____

____

____

____

____

II. Terms. All other terms, conditions, statements, and requests of the Last Will shall remain in effect. In every respect, I hereby ratify, reaffirm and republish my Last Will dated the ____ day of ____________________, 20____.

IN WITNESS whereof I, the Testator, have authorized this Codicil on the undersigned date and in the presence of ☐ Two (2) Witnesses ☐ Two (2) Witnesses and a Notary Public.

Testator's Signature ____________________ Date ______________, 20____

Print Name ____________________

I declare, as Witness, the Testator executed this Codicil in my presence.

Witness Signature ____________________ Date ______________, 20____

Print Name ____________________

I declare, as Witness, the Testator executed this Codicil in my presence.

Witness Signature ____________________ Date ______________, 20____

Print Name ____________________

NOTARY ACKNOWLEDGMENT

County/Parish of ______________________ }

State of ______________________ }

A notary public or other officer completing this certificate verifies only the identity of the individual who signed the document to which this certificate is attached, and not the truthfulness, accuracy, or validity of that document.

On this ____ day of ______________________, 20____ personally appeared the

Testator, known as ________________________ [Testator's Name], of this Codicil and

acknowledged the foregoing to be (his/her) free act and deed, before me.

Notary Public Signature ________________________

Print Name ________________________

My Commission Expires: ________________

(Seal)

NOTES

NOTES

NOTES

NOTES

Made in the USA
Monee, IL
08 November 2026

68002051R00079